T0077941

ENERGY IS POWER

RAISE YOUR BODIES VIBRATIONAL ENERGY TO
A HEALTHIER MIND, BODY AND SOUL

HOLLY HARRELL

BALBOA.PRESS
A DIVISION OF HAY HOUSE

Balboa Press books may be ordered through booksellers or by contacting:

Balboa Press
A Division of Hay House
1663 Liberty Drive
Bloomington, IN 47403
www.balboapress.com
844-682-1282

Print information available on the last page.

ISBN: 978-1-9822-6966-1 (sc)
ISBN: 978-1-9822-6967-8 (e)

Balboa Press rev. date: 06/02/2021

CONTENTS

DEDICATION

I dedicate this book to my parents, Sam and Sally, Harrell. They have given me the best childhood ever. They have always backed me up throughout the ups and downs of my life and have given me the support and encouragement to move forward toward a better life.

ACKNOWLEDGMENT

I want to take a moment to send gratitude to my loving daughter, who supported me through this journey of becoming an author. Kat is a very gifted writer and was a huge help guiding me through writing my book.

My sons, Tommy and Eddie, have also been my greatest cheerleaders. They always support all my extraordinary adventures. This book has been a long-time goal and thank you both for all your love and support.

A special thanks goes out to the School of Metaphysics. The amazing education I acquired from there has opened my eyes to living a high-energy and holistic path that enables a fulfilling and worthwhile journey of life.

ABOUT THE AUTHOR

Power is Energy was developed through a lifetime of searching to find out how to master our own body's energy field. I knew deep down it was the answer to healing oneself and others., How do I master my energy flow to have a better life?

My whole life, I have been sensitive to energy vibrations of every kind. All my life, I've had a strong drawing to help people in need. I sense people's feelings, emotions, pain, or love just by being near them. I can feel loved one's feelings from far away. When someone is thinking about me, they pop into my mind or sometimes appear as if they are near me. I have always been susceptible to all vibrational energy around me.

Throughout childhood, I had a close friend who was sensitive like me. We would play games with our psychic ability like "read my mind," or searching for spirits to feel their energy, or walking through old vacant homes to find ghosts. I could feel them easily. They were chilly, and the energy was intense. We would try to talk to them. I did not understand how to talk to them because I only receive vibrations. It was hard to convert them into words. I realized that I was able to see and feel multi-dimensional energy. I thought it was just fun.

Dreams would come to me both good and horrible as premonitions to warn me of upcoming events, a disaster, or help a close one. It was to guide me through life. Sometimes, intense dreams or times of psychic overload were to instantly stop me from what I was doing to come to the aid of a family member or friend who was going through trauma. Other dreams were of significant events and times coming to me in my life. All my dreams have come true. I believe it is because I have seen and felt them and knew they were coming. I never knew how or when. I just knew it would happen. I have seen all my kids and see them clearly in their future.

I always have wanted to help the suffering and heal people. I can see and feel multi-dimensional spirits, the energy of many kinds, angels, past and future energy, met different entities. They are extremely high vibrational entities living with us and help guide us. Maybe a God. They visit me often, and sometimes I can see them if I can quiet down the brain enough.

In my young adult life, many premonitions would come to me. I would have a weird kind of out of the body, uncomfortable feeling come to me when this would happen. I would stop in the direction I was going and need to go to a different safe place. I always went home and waited it out until I would get the sight of what is happening. One time in college, I was at a book store waiting for my boyfriend to go to his college across town. I started to feel horrible vibrations and felt bad. When he came to get me, I said I have to go home, something is very wrong. He was so mad, but I refused to go in the direction we were to go. When at home, he was mad, and I was crying. He turned on the TV, and the news bulletin came out of a racial riot and massive killing of white people on the road we would have driven at that time. We would have been one of the many that got brutally murdered. He realized I saved both our lives that day. I have many more of these kinds of times.

I have a lifetime of stories of how I have come to understand vibrational energy and how important it is to understand the magnificence of its ability to help us be happier, healthier, safer, and more loving lives.

A spirit told me in my 20's I need to live life and experience life's of up and downs to offer my wisdom and help heal the world. Sometimes my world would be really dark and very painful, and I would not understand why I have to go through all this pain. Many people have come into my world with lots of fear and pain. I instantly would ride the path with them and help them work through the trauma to get them back on their feet and living life again. When I would learn the lesson, I would then understand healing in that kind better. I have helped many different people come from very dark egos, emotional pain to living a life of joy. I have walked the road with them, and that has shown me pain and understanding. I have seen death. I am a cancer survivor. I have helped many disturbed people find life instead of death, and I have changed my course to save myself from trauma.

These low vibrational times all have had a purpose. Each has shown me different life energy vibrations and how they can be healed and raised to live your life's path. I have always given unconditional love and have been able to see each person's soul. This has been tough on me throughout life because I always see the beauty in each person's soul and not their current conditioned ego. I have learned to look at both the soul and the current body, mind, and spirit today. This is how my book has come to me. I have been searching for the "why" in my life, and the light bulb came on when I dove into metaphysics and vibrational energy. It all came together on how everything, mind, body, and soul, all need to heal together to raise our bodies vibrations and get the rewards of a great life.

Law of attraction, miracles, your higher power will give you total peace or bliss. It will all come to you. Healing your wounds, being at peace, eating healthy, exercising, and seeing other energy fields comes too. I see so many adults searching and not finding the answer to energy vibrations to give them a high vibrational life. I see so many readying high-level spiritual books looking for the answer and not getting it. I see so many following the perfect diet and still die of a disease.

I want to teach people that you have to start from the inside by raising your body's vibrational energy and not to look for the answers on the outside. I have found four groups that all have to work together to have a high healthy vibrational body – your mind (also called ego), the foods you put in your body, the way you move your body (exercise), and your soul (higher power).

Follow me, and I will show you how.

PREFACE

My passion throughout my whole life has been to figure out how our bodies energy force can be understood to live a better life. I knew at a young age that I could feel many energy forces at many different levels. The fascination to learn and even master how to control our own energy force has been my dream. Throughout life many levels of awaking came to me about how we can control our bodies energy and use it to heal and live an amazing life. The issue was that I could not separate the ego or emotions from the soul's energy. I thought both were the same, and so, my ego ruled my path for a long time. I read books after books, tried all kinds of modalities to find the answer to how I could be at peace and understand my own energy force.

Dreams also have been a big part to how the higher powers or God would talk to me. I have had many premonitions or guiding dream through out my whole life. These dreams have been extremely helpful in guiding me or comforting me or even telling me how energy work. One amazing dream came to me at the start of my understanding of our own energy force in this world today. My dream told me that we have lived many lives in a state of ego and emotional controlling worlds. It has created many levels of blocking our energy from flowing. I asked to show me how can I get past this and have my complete power. My dream told me it will be extremely hard to release all negative energy block in my body in this lifetime. I could work toward healing, but harnessing the full power of our soul and body would not happen. In the dream it did show me the feeling of what full energy power would feel like. It was the most amazing feeling. I knew some day I would understand how to get to this level.

Learning metaphysics and learning from the best I came to realize I had total control to raise my energy force. The mastering the understanding of our body's energy force came to me. I realized that there were several parts to understand. Diet is a huge and essential part of the journey; it's what we eat. Exercise and movement is everything. The big one was learning about our ego and how we have lived a life of letting our emotions control us. That was my big turning point to not let my ego and conditioned emotions have control. Then the learning to connect with my higher power and understand getting out of the ego and letting life's energy and path guild us. Learning to talk to your angles, guilds, God is so empowering. This led me to create a 4-pillar plan to raise my whole mind, body and soul's energy force. It has been a game changer for sure. My life is absolutely amazing today.

INTRODUCTION

Hello, all you beautiful people, my name is Holly Harrell, and today I'm sharing with you something that I have been passionate about all my life. Something incredibly close to my heart. I have a major need to assist the young and old, those searching for ways to raise their own personal energies to live better lives and make their time on earth more meaningful and fulfilling. It is all about the energy force each of us possesses. The world is vibrating higher, and young folks today are trying hard to understand how they can connect to their own higher being. My knowledge comes from David Hawkins, Edgar Casey, School of Metaphysics, and Quantum Physics. Everything is centered on comprehending energy and learning how to master your energy. You will watch miracles happen when your mind, body, and soul are all vibrating healthy and high.

Through my life's search to live at a higher level of vibrational energy living, I have found how vibrational energy flow affects our lives in mind, body, and soul. It was indeed an epiphany that I had a little over 25 years ago. My first experience and understanding of how energy works in our bodies and lives dawned on me while reading Celestine's prophesy. The first time I learned—through a rather lovely story—about how energy works in this world and how we have learned to take advantage of others by robbing it from them. The literature elaborated on achieving a much higher level of vibration and live amazing, loving lives. I have spent my entire life in search of the invisible energy force that exists around us. I always knew it was the basis of all existence, and it is the means to live a loving life full of miracles truly.

Growing up, I always could feel and see invisible energy forces. I have not only been able to see spirits and energy flows but have also had powerful and pointed premonitions, the kind that has saved lives. Most importantly, I feel everything and everyone's emotions deeply. I always said my issue was possessing the ability to see others' souls sooner than later – and all souls are beautiful in their way. Due to this ability and inner notion, I would trust folks that had, in a sense, lost touch with their souls and only lived in their ego and conscious minds, something that got me in a lot of trouble. This can be very scary and emotionally tough as you grow up being hypersensitive to all life's energy. My mission path was shown to me at a young age to understand how this vibrational energy worked and all the intricacies that went with it. I have researched the subject for several years.

I developed a strong spiritual path to understand the unique levels of energy, spirits, other people's energy and grow into a higher, more advanced spiritual being or continuously evolve. During my younger years, in my meditations, I was told that I needed to live life's ups and downs to get a proper grip on vibrational energy and its effects on us. I have successfully managed to live through some tough times, and thankfully each time, I grew stronger. My difficult experiences made me understand what self-healing is and how we can heal our inner selves. It's fantastic to have the ability to recognize your pain and show yourself the way to get out of the darkness.

After achieving a healing body, you will enjoy the life waiting for you; peaceful, loving, and healthy. This understanding of the four pillars of vibrational energy will help you take full control of your life via a simple explanation of how your bodies vibrate at various levels to cater to different experiences. It is essential to understand your diet's bearing, what shape you are, how you handle stresses and emotional pain to have your body's energy rise. There is an emphasis placed on higher power and meditation. The higher you vibrate, the more extraordinary your life will be. I have miracles happen to me every day. The law of attraction is just part and parcel of my life. It is mind-blowing to connect to a higher state of being.

And by the way, it is not at all about money; it is about your body's vibrational level. It's possible to raise your body's vibrational energy to a fuller and happier life. Make dreams happen daily.

CHAPTER 1

HOW TO RAISE YOUR BODY'S VIBRATIONAL ENERGY FOR A HEALTHIER & HAPPIER LIFE

It has been centuries since people have struggled to become the best versions of themselves, elevate to a higher being, and have full control of their lives. There are goals of achieving the things mentioned above, and there is a sheer lack of knowledge and understanding of all the elements at play. Maybe you are someone struggling, facing the same problems and pain over and over. Let me tell you something; never think of yourself as alone. This journey of life is only as incredible as you choose to make it. It can be difficult at first, but with wisdom, enlightenment, and a conscious effort to become better, you will be rewarded.

This book is penned down to help bridge the gap between the old way of thinking and the new way many of us live today. It will ensure that you understand the laws of nature, energy, and the connection to God and how it connects us to our mind, body, soul, and nutrition. It seeks to allow the next generation to learn self-control to actively take charge of their own lives, world, and very souls. As a result, the world will become happier and healthier. This following chapter will dive into a discussion about vibrational energy and its significance in our lives. I aspire to help everyone not to be afraid of their higher vibrational gifts. Energies are present everywhere, so it's only a matter of time until your eyes are open wide enough to see and recognize them.

Young adults today are so aware and so open to a better world. I am here to help you take the necessary steps, manifest your goals, live your dreams, heal all wounds, raise your vibration, love life, be joyous, and stay focused. As you flip the pages of this book, imagine me as a subtle guiding light, gently urging your forward, helping you find your own way out of the darkness. The blessings that come with living a life that you don't need an escape from are endless. You may have some questions in your head right now, such as; what is VE? How can we raise our VE? How did the world become so horrible and unhealthy, why are we vibrating so low, and so forth? Please do not worry and allow me to put those thoughts to rest. Soon, you will come to realize that the answer at the base of it all is quite simple; any persisting problems can be fixed by raising your vibrational energy.

Vibrational Energy

Vibrational energy is associated with a meditative practice related to spirituality. However, this is far from some kind of ungrounded pseudo-science. This practice certainly connects to the wellness world and cultivates a healthy mind rooted in physics. Might I add, Einstein taught us that everything is energy; hence every single person, place, and thing vibrates at a specific frequency. High vibrational energy is known as the energy that is strong and good. This energy is pure, and it can come from whatever you wish to call it, such as universe energy, source energy, or God energy. On the other hand, low vibration energy is dark, dull, and feels extremely heavy. It is associated with unpleasant emotions, for instance, suffering, anger, or fear.

Now, based on this intel, you are advised to raise your vibration. Raising your vibration reflects that you have self-awareness of your emotions, thoughts, and spirituality. When you're well aware of these, you will be able to recognize your vibrations and actively do something to shift yourself into a high-vibrational state. Before I get into the importance of vibrational energy, I would like to first talk about vibration. After all, your vibration is what sets and exudes your vibrational energy. You see, it's essential for you to come to terms with what is being said here. Only then will you be able to practice what I am preaching.

What is Vibration?

'Vibration' is a fancy word to describe your overall state of being. Everything in the universe is made up of energy vibrating at different frequencies. Even things that appear solid are made up of vibrational energy fields at the quantum level. And this includes you too. Judging from a scientific and metaphysical perspective, we are simply beings made up of various energy levels. These energy levels are mental, physical, spiritual, and emotional. Each of these levels has a vibrational frequency which altogether combines to create your overall vibration of being.

Vibrations are known to operate at both high and low frequencies, within us and all around us. It will be evident if your vibration is low. All it takes is bringing awareness to your situation and then carefully working on rectifying it. Maybe money no longer flows, your health is poor, or you feel surrounded by a group of negative people. On the contrary, when your vibration is higher, you will experience a beautiful sense of living in the flow. When things are in proper flow or alignment, you will be jumping out of bed every day filled with optimism, you will be befriending positive, inspiring people, life will be heading in the right direction, and your bank balance might just also be fantastic! Other people may assume that you have all the luck in the world. Although, in reality, you will have invited in all these blessings on your own.

You must have heard that energy attracts energy. Let me tell you a story to explain this better. The vibration of one of my best friends was low on a particular day. She told me that it felt like she was trapped in a cage; nothing in her life that day seemed to go right. As one bad thing followed another, negative thoughts clouded her mind. The point here is that when your vibration is low, all areas of your life will be impacted in some way or the other. It is like a chain reaction, a domino effect.

However, if your vibration is high, you are more likely to attract the positive, motivating people into your life that you desire; you will feel alert and active; things will transpire in your favor; opportunities seem to fall in your lap.

Importance of Vibrational Energy

Have you ever heard people talking about and wanting to attain a higher vibration? Or are you unsure of what that means or why it's important to you? In the following section, I will address both questions for you to have a clearer understanding and hopefully motivate you to attain higher vibrational energy for yourself/your life. Each one of us vibrates energetically at a certain frequency. The lower the frequency, the denser your energy, and the heavier your problems may seem. Here you may experience sorrow and discomfort in your physical body, experience heavy emotions as well as mental confusion. Psychically, your energy is darker. You need to exert a great deal of effort to achieve your goals. As a result, overall, your life takes on a negative quality.

On the other hand, the higher your energy's frequency or vibration, the lighter you feel in your physical, mental, and emotional bodies. You experience more substantial personal power, peace, love, joy, and clarity. You will have little to no discomfort or pain, if any, in your physical and mental body. As for heavy emotions, they will be dealt with quickly and smoothly. Your energy in this state pulsates with light. Your life flows in synchronization, and you manifest what you desire effortlessly. Overall, your life takes on a positive quality. Moving on, being in a higher vibration will become more important to you and the rest of the world as we experience further awareness of the polarities between the lower and higher vibrations. We will start to perceive a greater separation between the dark and the light, and there will be a need for us to consciously choose between dark/light and higher/lower vibrations.

We are moving to a higher vibrational frequency in our everyday world currently. It is common for our youth to see and experience different dimensional perspectives. They are all raising the bar and are way more open to higher energy fields. This, in turn, opens them up to healthier and happier existences. I am sharing with you the secret to how you can get past life's pains and live a happier, healthier life by raising your vibrational energy. Live your chosen path. Do you want to feel great all the time, not be affected by downers and control freaks, handle daily living happier, see and feel your path happening, or help people instead of hurting yourself and others? Do you want to know why some people are so happy, and everything just happens perfectly for them? It's all about your body's vibrational energy. How is it that so many individuals are just happy, successful, focused, and accomplishing great things in their lives all the time? You can too, and I will show you just how by raising your body's vibrational energy field. I aim to show you how vibrational energies are affected by our diet, exercise, emotions, people around us, and our God.

The significance of vibrational energy is as follows. First and foremost, your emotional well-being matters. Have you ever noticed how some people always seem to land on their feet, whereas others are plagued by bad luck and struggle? There is a direct link between a person's emotional well-being, energetic frequency, and overall life experience. Even though we live in the same world, our experiences and outlook on life depend on our energetic vibration. People who have higher vibrational energy enjoy a far more empowered and positive view of life. They tend to work on a deep love-based emotional level.

Additionally, such people can often see solutions to life's challenges with utmost clarity and identify opportunities when knocking on their door. Those who vibrate on a lower-level experience more negative emotions. Sadly, their vibrational level ensures that they mainly experience struggle and strife. Therefore, you see if you actively pursue well-being and emotional health, you will be able to enjoy the energetic advantages of love, optimism, and happiness.

Secondly, what you place your attention on matters a lot. Your activities, hobbies, and past times resonate at different energetic levels. In simpler words, this means the TV shows, books and hobbies you place your attention on, drawing the energy of that activity into your own space. Choosing to watch an uplifting TV show, reading inspiring books, and partaking in hobbies that bring you utmost joy will make it easier to create a positive outlook on life. It is important to "feed" and "nourish" your head and soul. A famous, ancient cultural example of this can be found in traditional Chinese custom. In China, it is believed that a pregnant woman passes all experiences through the eyes, by the heart, and into the growing baby. Thus, she is encouraged to enjoy only pleasant environments and activities. Similarly, to get our best sense of well-being, we must try to do the same.

Thirdly, what you project outwards also can't be undermined. This concept refers to the incredible energetic impact that your words, thoughts, and intentions can have on the world around us. A relevant way to understand this is through the story regarding ice crystals and how they can take a beautiful form or an irregular—ugly—form. When polite, kind, and loving prayers were made in the presence of water, exquisite patterns were created. On the flip side, when the water was exposed to aggression, cruel intentions, and violence, it disturbingly took the form of polluted and muddied crystals. Likewise, your thoughts are electrical impulses in your present. Your words are a product of the vibration of your voice in the air. You must realize the impact you have on the people and world around you, and your being is invisible yet inescapable. Remember what you think, say, and project outwardly into the world will make it healthy or unhealthy.

Lastly, who you decide to spend your time with can't be ignored either. You are quite profoundly affected on an energetic level by the people in your environment. We have all met people who instantly lift our mood and those who bring us crashing down. This is not only because of personalities; it is due to their vibrational levels. If you are looking to enjoy a more positive outlook, you must let yourself make a mindful decision about who you spend your time with. Keeping and staying in the company of like-minded, positive people will help lift your vibration, which will draw more positive people into your circle. It's high time that you walk away from destructive relationships and toxic people.

The Four Pillars

Our body's vibrational energy flow affects our health and mental state. Your mind, body, and soul are all affected by four pillars: diet, exercise, emotions or ego, your higher power. These four pillars all go together and impact how high vibrational our body's vibrating and healing. These four pillars cover everything from our diet and physical health to our egos or emotions, relationships, connection to the divine, or our higher being. I have designed a four-pillar plan to help each part move to higher vibrational energy—the medical world today versus the holistic approach we are moving towards. The medical world is all about dealing with the problem and just giving you chemicals to handle, mask or poison to heal. Western medicine views the human body as a machine and not as the delicate holistic environment that it really is!

The main issue here is how we got to this problem. Where did it come from to start within your body? What is breaking down in your body to create the medical issue? Dealing with the medical issue with the current "Doctor approach" is like putting a bandage on a gash. We need to get to the underlying problem to get the body back healing itself. Your health and happiness are all tied to your diet, exercise, ego or emotions, and your higher power.

My goal is to help you understand quite literally how we can take control of our own life and body. To show you how natural energy vibrations work on the Mind-body and soul. If you give a flower a lot of water, nutrition, and sunlight, it will grow strong and healthy. A flower that has no water, no care, and no sun will not live. We are very much the same, but extraordinarily complex.

I have learned to understand that energy vibrations affect our body in numerous ways. The way we eat and give our body nutrition. The way we take care of our bodies through exercise. The way our emotions, minds, and relationships with others significantly affect us through our ego. Probably the most important is how close you are to your higher source or God. All these pillar areas Diet, Exercise, Ego/mind, and God are all very much needed to be understood if you want to learn how they raise or lower the vibrational energy within your body.

The ego is lower vibration energy and causes harm to the body. Lack of physical strength and oxygen affects our ability to move bad stuff out of our bodies. This makes the body hold onto toxicity and poison, which in time it starts damaging us. The ego and feelings relating to it can be extremely tricky and are associated with heavy vibrations. Guilt, apathy, grief, fear, disappointment, hate, scorn, blame, and others originate in the ego, not in the logical brain. These emotions come from conditioning in your past.

Would you like to be at an energy level that your body naturally cures itself? Where cancer, diabetes, and heart disease can't manifest? Is your body at a vibrational level that facilitates healing? This is a stage where your body can naturally heal and rebuild itself. At this level, it will rebuild to a new stronger, healthy, and loving body. While staying physically fit, eating clean and healthy is the primary key to keeping the body vibrating in a full healing mode. Learning to move through your emotions to guide you and not to control you is also key. Fear, selfishness, guilt, apathy, grief, anger, and pride are going to be a part of your life. Learning how to heal and move past your fears and past pains is what you need to do. We don't want to let our emotions control our world. We just guide us to make the best decision to follow our path.

Did you know the ego or emotions are not part of the brain? They are outside the brain and are all part of how we have been conditioned. This means we can learn to be loving, happy, and high vibrational.

How to Increase your Body's Vibrational Energy

So how do we raise our vibration? I know it sounds very complex, but I'm here not to tell you, but instead, simplify it for you. The answer lies in the activities that you do. Read on to learn how you can start attracting more abundance in your life and vibrate higher.

Become Conscious of Your Thoughts

Everything you think, say, or feel ends up becoming your reality. Every thought that comes into your head has an impact on you, whether you realize it or not. When you change those unpleasant thoughts for the positive, your reality is likely to become positive too. Of course, it's a whole lot easier said than done in the face of adversity. But how about the next time a displeasing thought enters your head, you take the time to acknowledge it, thank it for showing up, and then just dismiss it. You need to continuously turnaround from all sorts of negativity and let your life fill up with positivity.

Eat well

Some foods vibrate at exceedingly high frequencies, and some at lower ones. If you consume foods covered in chemicals and pesticides or foods found within plastic packaging, it will most certainly leave you vibrating lower. Contrariwise, devour good quality organic produce, food as nature intended it, and feel the high vibrations disseminate throughout your body. Most importantly, pay close attention to how eating certain foods make you and your body feel.

Find clarity

To manifest something into your life, you have to first have a clear vision of what it is and what it looks like. Clarity can pave the way for you to open your mind and heart. Thus, begin to imagine the reality of having what you say you want to attain. After you have that clarity, lean into the feeling of already having it to uncover any subconscious blocks that might hold you back from gaining it.

Journal Your Vision

To get an instant vibrational boost, there is a practice called scripting. This entails journaling about what you wish to invite into your life as if you already have it. Describe all your visions in detail, like a movie script, and include how the sensation of having it feels. Be very thorough. This will help you elevate your vibration to align with that what you want.

Be Kind and Loving To Yourself

How you talk to yourself or care for yourself must not be ignored. The messages and thoughts that you give to yourself directly impact how you feel. Treat yourself the same way as you would treat someone you dearly love. This translates into ditching the negative self-talk and nourishing yourself with polite, compassionate words. Start today. Start somewhere, even if you have to fake it at first. Eventually, you will get into the practice of it.

Connect to A Higher Power

Connecting to a higher power of your choice is undoubtedly a powerful way to boost your vibration. One of the most crucial parts about connecting to some sort of higher power is feeling like you are protected and not alone. It assists you to get into a different realm, and it helps you to ground yourself.

When you increase your vibrational energy, you will have a loving life. You will get to experience miracles daily. Ego or negative emotions from others will not seem to bother you and will go away rapidly. God, or your higher power, will be felt so close that a kind of happy, content feeling will come over you, and all worries about life's troubles will go away. Answers to your life's direction will come to you quickly through visions and clues to guide you to your chosen path. Healing from past traumas and life's uncomfortable experiences all need to be brought to the surface and healed. We will need to learn how to feel through negative emotions, discover the message they may hold, and let them go. The more we let go of our pains and fears, the freer we will be to vibrate at a higher level. This takes time and will need to be guided through help from others. The feeling of knowing we do not have to be in pain or fear ever is so enlightening.

CHAPTER 2

WHY RAISE OUR VIBRATIONAL ENERGY?

In the previous chapter, you learned what vibrational energy is and about its importance in our lives. In the following chapter, I will be diving into a discussion on the need to increase your vibrational energy to lead a happier life, along with a brief discussion on energy flow. I seek to help you understand the vibrational energy side of your mind and emotions. You will be surprised to know how they affect and control your life. I will teach you stuff about your body's diet and nutrition and show you how your body's fitness level and H2O levels are vital. Not to mention, I will also be instilling the significance of having an excellent soul connection to the divine/universal source of power. Earlier, we learned that all four pillars are equally important in your life. You can't do one or two parts, avoiding the third or fourth.

All are compulsory to ensure that you vibrate higher overall, and trust me when I say this, the same is immensely beneficial. In my opinion, most of us are not living our best lives right now. We are not living up to our potential, to be the absolute best versions of ourselves. We can indeed live better, do more, and be happier. We have the supreme power to change our current reality and attract what we desire. To do that, we must raise our vibration to match the vibration of what we wish to attract. With that being said, there are different levels of vibrational being. You must let go of the stories you have been telling yourself all this time. We need to stop playing the role of the victim.

It is time to observe your thoughts from a vantage point rather than attaching emotions to them.

Here's how you can understand changing your perspective from negative to positive. For the most part, we all have lived in a world where life's conditioning and our reactive emotions have led us through life. We sometimes feel negative or painful, and we are trained to react to that impulse. We learn to bury our feeling or react violently. How many people do you know always talk about how horrible their lives are and never get better? I have lived in a repetitive circle of similar people but different spots. All have selfish intent for their own ego or pleasure. They really have not seen me for who I am or love me for me. They always want me to be something else. My ego and emotional state want to believe they genuinely love me, but the stomach red flag is always there. Why do I always feel something is wrong? Then the problem happens, and I get so mad at myself for falling for the same controlling ego-based people. Today, I have worked through many levels of personal growth times, and it feels great to be in control of my own life. You can see through fake people. You even can stop the negative reaction of living that leads us to a terrible ending.

Alter your environment for the greater good, be kind to yourself, be mindful of who or what you listen to, what you fuel your body with, and who you choose to spend your valuable time with. I can understand how it's tempting to succumb to a feeling of helplessness concerning the future of the planet and all its inhabitants. But I assure you that channeling your efforts into raising your vibrational frequency is one of the most outstanding gifts you can give to the world. When you decide to lift yourself, you tend to motivate others and bring them into your circle. This happens to be the only way you can contribute to raising the collective consciousness of the world. After all, it's the little droplets of water that form an ocean. Similarly, you can start today and play your part. Raise your vibrational energy to live a far more loving, peaceful, and joyous life.

The Need of Raising our Vibrational Energy

It is becoming quite clear to most of us that working together with kindness, acceptance, and compassion are the main missing pieces for resetting humanity's fast and furious trajectory into separation and division. It has become far more apparent that we cannot create solutions from the same consciousness level that spawn the very problems we are looking to address. Raising our vibration for drawing peaceful solutions is an undertaking that calls for gentleness, forgiveness, and inclusive love that respects our differences.

I passionately believe that there's a particular purpose behind everything meaningful in life. For instance, when you want to address your physical fitness, you change your food and lifestyle habits. You resort to more physical activities and consuming more nutritious foods. You could make exercise a key part of your daily routine. Likewise, increasing your vibrational energy takes making certain changes. To put it simply, we need to increase our vibrational energy to lead a life of contentment in every aspect. We are aware of how our thoughts and intentions can have profound effects on the world around us. Plants are known to react negatively to malicious intentions. On the contrary, sending love and energy to a warm cup of tea can improve the mood of someone who drinks it.

Therefore, raising your vibration is as simple as becoming mindful of your intentions and choosing to only live through love and compassion. The outcome of high vibrational energy is spectacular, so without further ado, let's get right into it. When you make the intention to spread kindness, the more harmonious your life will become. It's not only just a psychological effect. Instead, the whole world around you will respond to your energy. You have a tremendous power to shift your world and the world of others. You may not always be able to change someone's mind or behavior on the spot, but you can certainly decide to live in a path of light and love, positively affecting people.

When poised in your higher vibration, you experience several benefits. Decisions and solutions flow more quickly due to increased access to your heart's intuitive wisdom. Discernment becomes more inclusive; choices become more transparent and effective. It is a lot simpler to deflect anxiety, frustration, impatience, and other chronic stress producers that immensely strain our critical thinking and reasoning. In a higher vibrational composure, most of us feel more self-secure. Moving on, when your vibrational energy raises, so does your vitality, well-being, and wholeness. You will soon realize how you feel alert, important, and focused. As a result, the things that felt missing are replaced with a stronger sense of being. I am sure that the things mentioned above are goals most of you wish to achieve.

We crave mental, emotional, and physical abundance in our lives, and what better way to attain those than by raising our vibrational energy? With the removal of lower vibrational energies, your thoughts, emotions, and spiritual awareness are known to function more optimally. Each of them is balanced and works in combination with the other. This is achieved by removing blockages and negative energies by raising your vibration. You will also notice a greater awareness of your spiritual gifts. This translates into the higher your vibration is, the stronger your connection will be with the energies around you. Your spiritual gifts will enhance your vibration. In addition to this, with your vibrational energy rising, you will acquire spiritual grounding.

Spiritual grounding may sound like an odd reason to raise your vibration. Although when you raise your vibration, you strengthen your connection with mother earth. You feel more connected and grounded. This, in turn, may reduce overthinking and the feeling of being separate from life. Lastly, let's not forget how essential self-empowerment and personal development are. To ensure these, we must raise our vibrational energy to its full capacity. To feel fully empowered is probably one of the most life-changing experiences since you know who you are, what your power is, what exactly you want, and how in-tune you are with the world around you. Raising your vibration boosts this and helps with your personal development goals through the spiritual alignment and removal of negative energies.

Judging from a spiritual well-being point of view, the need to raise your vibrational energy is undeniable since the benefits are immense. What I see for tomorrow is simple. I want to assist the youth in becoming comfortable with their higher vibrational gifts without fear and judgment. These gifts are everywhere and all around us. In fact, I can see that some of the youths are already so aware, so open, and welcoming to the possibility of a better world. Those under 40 are starting to vibrate at a higher frequency level as a normal part of life. This helps us collectively stop living a reactionary ego-based existence and move to a healthier position, which encourages our body to heal and grow. This is fantastic because we will be moving into the near future where today's doctors, along with all their horrible masking, symptom-focused medicine, will be left in the past.

Hospitals and doctors will be mostly in the health and wellness department. Preventative Doctors and hospitals will be the replacement. Future doctors will be holistic, energy healers, pathologists, and nutritional counselors, and fewer emergency rooms will be needed. I am here to aid you in taking steps to realize and manifest your dreams, heal your deepest wounds, raise your vibration, love the life you live, and be joyous and focused. I want you to learn how your mind, body, and soul are equally imperative in your life. You can't skip anything and expect a higher balanced energy force.

The Outcome of Raising Vibrational Energy

The effect of raising your VE higher will be that you will radiate in a way that exudes peace and wellness towards all. As for those who cannot handle your new higher, happier self you will observe them organically removing themselves from your sphere – likely for the better. Negativity will no longer have access to you. It will cease to be a part of your world. You will attract happier, like-minded, and kinder people. Your work will be your path, and love will get you up each day. It will be nothing less than floating down a river of life instead of climbing a mountain from hell.

Your ego reactions will just flow through you, and you will have the utmost control of them. There will be observance and no response to them. You will be able to process them, address them if need be from a place of curiosity, and then let them go. You will stay in a happier state of existence, and you will have control over your happiness. No one will be able to control your life except for you. I have hundreds of examples of how miracles have happened in my life. Clues are shown to me daily. I manifest my dreams and my destiny through the law of attraction. I can mediate with higher frequencies. Money and wealth are not at all my driving force. Instead, my life, family, helping others, doing well, and my dreams are my path.

I want you to have faith in what I say because I come from a place of learning. I was once just like you, lost in the chaos of the world, struggling to find some direction, reclaim my heart, body, mind, and soul. The keenness and willingness to have better allowed me to acquire information on the subject in question and spread the word. I hope to light you up and make you believe in all the beautiful possibilities in existence.

Factors that Cause Disruption in the Flow of Energy

The flow of energy is your energy and how it moves through every part of your body. Your thoughts, emotions, and actions can have either a positive or negative impact on energy flow. Have you ever noticed how when something doesn't go right, you get upset? Then you carry that energy within you and project it consciously or subconsciously into the world and others around you. On the other hand, when you're filled with positivity and synonymous with being a bundle of joy, your energy flow is also positive. You remain happy and sprinkle it on others present in your company.

There are a couple of factors that can disrupt the flow of energy. You may not even realize just how fast they can alter your energy flow. The following are some factors that unfortunately cause a disturbance in the flow of energy:

- Negative emotions such as anger, stress, guilt, anxiety, depression, jealousy, and hatred.

- Toxic behaviors you indulge in or project upon others
- Drugs and Alcohol
- Poor dietary habits
- Lack of motivation or willingness to achieve your goals

Assignment: Food for Thought

Now that you have some insight and clarity on energy flow, I would like you to take some time from your busy schedules and ponder over something crucial. Review your own energy, look at your issues carefully, and reflect on how negative energy or low energy affects your life. Once you figure out all the above, get to work. Make some necessary changes for your growth and rise gracefully. I believed in myself, and now I believe in you to excel, be the supreme being you were created to be, and live your life to the fullest.

CHAPTER 3

WHAT IS YOUR ENERGY FLOW?

Everything is energy. Learning to curb the overall energy in your body constructively helps in maintaining elevated internal energy levels. '*Qi*' or '*chi*,' as Taz Bhatia explains, is the current energy that flows through the channels and passes through all the parts of the human body. This flow of energy provides the human body with circulation, nutrients, and minerals vital for survival. The flow of spiritual energy throughout the body is as essential as blood flow for human existence. Other schools of traditional medicines regard *Chi* as the ultimate measure of a person's vitality.

The Energy Flow

The human body's energy network is known as the meridian; the meridian line is the channel through which the energy flows and is transported throughout the human body. It can be thought of as the energy circulatory system.

The energy system of the human body can be compromised as a result of several reasons. Problems in sleeping patterns, scarcity of food, clean freshwater intake, and fresh air availability can disrupt the human body functions. Furthermore, having an imbalance in one's relationships can also harm our body's energy levels. Any blockages in the human body's energy flow cause negative impacts on a person's health; a person feels excessively fatigued, irritable, depressed, stress, muscular pain, or weak.

To have a healthy and fit life, they should work on maintaining their body energy. One should refrain from focusing on negative feelings, like guilt, revenge, anger, and hopelessness. This is the first step in filtering one's energy and keeping it free from toxins that poison a person's aura of internal peace.

According to Cayce, illnesses are birthed when the energy from one part is sucked out to make another part of the body active and healthy. This collateral damage occurs when a person starts to lose confidence in themselves and their mental and physical peace.

What does the Energy System Consist of?

Auras, chakras, and meridians are the components of the energy system within the human body. To you, these may appear to be the same. However, it is crucial to identify that these components may be intricately linked but have their significance in their way.

The Aura

Have you seen pictures and paintings of various spiritual leaders having a sort of halo or florescent radiance surrounding the head and sometimes the entire body? The fluorescent light represents the human Aura. Aura is our life force. The electromagnetic energy field flows and extends beyond the physical anatomy of living and non-living things. Even animals and plants have their aura, which helps them maintain their internal energy levels. The Human Aura comprises seven layers through which the energy flows into the human body from the surroundings and vice versa through auras and chakras. The aura is what forms the outermost layer that protects or preserves the energy in a human body. I regard aura as some warm cozy comforter that we cover our bodies with; it protects us from physical and mental harm.

A solid, healthy aura diminishes the probability of developing sickness, builds one's fascination with others, and resists toxins and contaminations. Negative energy, toxins, and contaminations in the surroundings initially enter the atmosphere before affecting the body. Regular cleaning of aura through positive healing eliminates them before they influence the body. Chakras and auras are intricately linked to one another.

Chakras

Chakras can be envisioned as circling pinwheels. We have seven chakra points, which manage the flow of energy throughout the endocrine system, based on what a person is thinking and feeling at any moment in time. Each of these points serves as energy transfers. Chakras can direct their energy to any point within the human body where it is needed. Chakras can be blocked, just as the human mind begins to get clogged when individuals are faced with adversity. You can also control and manage your emotional blockage by channeling chakras inside your own body!

Chakras and auras work hand in hand. You think and feel emotions every moment of every day, even if it is involuntary. When you reason with yourself and come up to conclusions on your own by weighing the pros and cons of the situations, your energy, aura, and chakras affect your energy. When your chakras are well aligned and flow effortlessly throughout your body, you feel positive and passionate. You have a clear trail of thoughts, which brings you eternal peace. Some days, it feels like the whole world is against you, doesn't it? Have you ever wondered why you feel so drained, both emotionally and physically, on such days? You have those days when everything feels off because you face a blockage of energy within your body. Your chakras are not as thorough as they had been in the good days. This harms your aura, dims it. Low levels of internal energy are induced because of negative thinking.

The different chakras are associated with different feelings within our bodies. The flow of energy in the *base chakra* is linked to humans' interpersonal needs, feelings of security and safety, and a strong feeling of self-identity. This chakra's energy can face obstruction in its flow when a person is dealing with broken relationships and is subjected to unreciprocated emotional energy, feeling low on self-esteem, or facing depression. Here, it is important to note that this impacts inner peace, but it also affects the physical human body. You can identify the missing ingredient if you have the following symptoms:

- Chronic pain in the lower back (This is where this chakra point is located)
- Digestive disorders
- Disorders dealing with immunity and fertility
- Obsessive-Compulsive Disorder (OCD)

If you feel low on your creativity and face problems with expressing your emotions and feeling, your sacral chakra needs some fixing. The Sacral Chakra is located just below the navel. Blockage in the sacral can make a person feel emotionally unstable, subject to depression and sexual dysfunction. Along with the emotional issues, the physical problems include:

- Constipation
- Stiffy Feeling in The Lower Back And Hips
- Kidney Problems
- Pelvic Pain

A perfect flow in this chakra makes a person feel self-sufficient, which projects high self-esteem and overall wellness. To clear this chakra off any negative energy, exercising is amazingly effective. The butterfly pose, cobra pose, goddess pose, and other hip-opening exercises can help unblock this chakra. People are also advised to eat nuts, sweet potatoes, mangoes, pumpkins, and other orange-colored foods. By balancing the energy in this chakra, you can feel a deeper connection with your acquaintances, boosting confidence.

Internal drive and feeling of self-reliance are dependent on Solar Plexus, the chakra point located below the breastbone. Tension, multitasking, and trauma from childhood can trigger imbalance in this chakra. Lack of stability in this chakra can cause a person to feel helpless and lose concentration. Other stress-induced disorders like phobias, eating, skin, and sleep disorders are also given birth due to disturbance in this energy level.

The Heart Chakra, located to the center of the chest, is the bridge that links the lower chakras to the upper one. Love and other emotions are felt through this chakra. Imbalance in this chakra makes a person age faster and can also cause heart diseases, respiratory disorders, and frequent infections.

The Throat Chakra controls all the bodily communications that individuals do with other beings. It can be imbalanced due to lack of communication or any existential trauma in an individual's upbringing.

The chakra point present in the center of the forehead, just above the eyebrows, is the Third-eye Chakra. Wisdom and psychic abilities are associated with this chakra. Furthermore, if this chakra is blocked, a person becomes indecisive, unable to follow what they want, and may find it hard to learn new skills.

The Crown Chakra is responsible for the connection individuals have with their higher self, and ultimately the higher being. It is located at the top of the head. It is linked to all other chakras in the human body. If the lower chakras in the human body are blocked, it is bound to cause interruptions in the flow of energy in this chakra. This chakra is so complex that it is not possible to achieve a complete flow of energy in this chakra for most people. The flow of energy in this chakra can be regulated by certain handpicked exercises, prayers, meditation, and moments of thankfulness and silence.

Chakras Can Direct Their Energy to Any Point Within The Human Body

Poisoning the Energy System

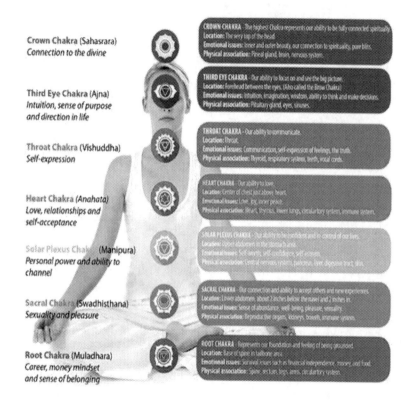

Crown Chakra (Sahasrara)
Connection to the divine

Third Eye Chakra (Ajna)
Intuition, sense of purpose and direction in life

Throat Chakra (Vishuddha)
Self-expression

Heart Chakra (Anahata)
Love, relationships and self-acceptance

Solar Plexus Chakra (Manipura)
Personal power and ability to channel

Sacral Chakra (Swadhisthana)
Sexuality and pleasure

Root Chakra (Muladhara)
Career, money mindset and sense of belonging

Humans function best when they are in a balanced environment. When we are subjected to toxicity, it damages the flow of energy within our bodies. The excessive use of harmful substances makes us lose touch with ourselves, which makes us feel broken from the inside. The human body is a very closed circuit; what happens in one part of the body affects the rest of the organs. The adverse impacts of drug use can also show up as a form of physical and mental disorders.

Drugs today are killing us. They disrupt the balance that is necessary for us to function well. Taking drugs is like putting a bandage on the issue, and no good comes out of it. The issues need to be dealt with rather than being put on the back burner. You should try and work on whichever issues you might be facing, as these take up the substantial mental space, which have a prominent effect on a person's mental peace, which subsequently impacts the energy levels of the human body. The stress that sits on a person's brain can be as dangerous as cancer for the human body. When a person indulges in alcoholism, the person suffers emotional trauma. People do not deal with emotional issues, and rather they seek a silent escape without dealing with it.

The usage of substances like cocaine and other drugs gives a person an emotional boost. Therefore they are so addicting; they make people feel good about themselves and escape their realities. People use drugs as a *shortcut* to feeling better about themselves by fleeing into a parallel world where they can avoid their real-life problems. The after-effects of drugs like cocaine are extraordinarily strong. These drugs alter the energy field of the human body. They have a drastic impact on the entire energy system.

Emotional Robbing of Today

In today's world, we have learned to rob each other's energy to get things done our way. We crave the feeling of ultimate power, and to achieve that level of power, we will cross whichever boundaries we face. People use manipulating techniques daily just to achieve a feeling of superiority. I think we have been accustomed to using these techniques without realizing the long-term impacts of such negative practices. People tend to manipulate others by making themselves look more innocent and helpless than they are. While other individuals intimidate others, bully them, and try to make the most out of the little power that has been given to them. We steal from each other to get the vital energy we need.

Mankind has developed a 3rd dimension of living in the ego-governed mind for a long time. We are taught to react through our emotions and conditioned by the life we live. It does not even cross your mind to think this emotion is to help me, not for me to react negatively and hurt other people. Wars, religious conflicts, and lifestyles have all been created by emotional ego knee jerky reactions. This was not the original purpose of utilizing this wonderful ability to feel and have emotions. Ego emotions are to guide us, not use them as a reason to hurt or control them.

How does energy stealing look and feel?

For some issues to be solved, the root of the issue needs to be found. This era's medical techniques are developed to 'cover-up' the problem, not to solve it. The society of today works on masking the issues rather than treating the source. People want to get to the top, and they are ready to do whatever it takes. We need to realize that where you are today is exactly where you are supposed to be. You need to give things time, and you should learn to embrace it, need to love it, and focus on diverting your energy to a positive and constructive path to get to elevated internal energy levels. You need to let the energy flow and make its way, not force it into any direction.

Energy stealing is quite interesting to watch. When you start understanding energy-robbing, you can literally sit back and just see it happen from one person to another. The person that is feeling low energy through illness, deep pains, and fear will think he needs to react harshly to another person, particularly on a bad day. Emotions, in this case, are just on the surface and the other person is the victim serving as a scapegoat to bring out this discomfort. The other person, on most occasions, is innocent but will soon be into the pain of the other. Funny enough, the innocent person often begins with better energy, standing strong with an aura that is radiating groundedness and strong balance. The other is weak and needs some of that great energy. We have done this energy-robbing for so long that society does not realize that this has become the normal way to get more energy. We steal from each other by hurting or manipulating. The aggressor jumps right into the other person's energy, and the vampire energy stealing begins. You can see the strong person's energy slip away as they become weaker and weaker. Their body language starts to slump over more and more; they may cross their arms around their chests to protect the heart chakra.

The vampire aggressor is usually feeling quite good by now and is standing higher and stronger. They usually can't stop till they have taken all they can take. This is amazing to watch. Kind of scary too. Just to remind you, this wonderful world has a great energy balance that we have lost by taking without returning and by disconnecting. The trees and outdoors provide us with the best vibrational energy. We need the energy of the outdoors to give us the vibrations our bodies need. We don't need ego-robbing energy from other people. We need to offer loving energy everywhere we go to help others.

The existence of energy vampires and energy biters is real. We have been robbing each other's energy for 1000s of years. We use our emotions to enter someone's aura or space, and we make them uncomfortable. We throw anger, fear, humiliation, anything to get the person feeling uncomfortable. This is energy-robbing. The person that is not feeling well will rob you of your energy. You will feel terrible and sometimes actually sick when they get through with you. It is very real. The best example is a husband comes home from work from a bad day. He walks into the home to a lovely wife and kids, ready to play with daddy. Except he is feeling bad from a horrible day at work. His boss was all over his case all day and energy-robbing all his energy. Since all we know is to react to our emotions, we pass them on and steal from the ones we love. Of course, he picks a fight. He will know how to get a good emotion out of everyone. He does not even realize that he is actually stealing all his loved ones' energy to feel better.

Have you had one of those friends who go from friend to friend till they wear out the friendship because they are so needy? It would be best if you said, "Stop. I cannot help you anymore," to set your boundaries, or you'll just get tired of everything being so horrible, story after story looking for pity from you. It is still vampires stealing your energy.

Take-away

I decided that it was time to change, and rightfully so, I did make a change. The take-away lesson from this time of my life is that you need to know when to stop letting others take advantage of your vulnerability. You need to take control of your life when you feel emotionally and physically drained because only you have the power to do that. You need to learn when to say no and take the reins of your life into your own hands and steer it to the path of peace.

Energy & Religion

Your spiritual energy is deeply impacted by the relationship you have with the higher being, i.e., God. In the world of today, spirituality is viewed as a shady voodoo, demon-taming practice. Society does not accept it. Individuals conform to a world of acceptance, pain, fear, and existence. People have no source of internal happiness. People are lost in the business of their lives and are caught up with daily life activities such that they do not have time to heal the relationship they have with God. People take religion as the mere robotic actions linked to religious activities; going to the church on Sundays is the most 'religious' one could be. People have taken the word of God extremely lightly. I assume many people have no idea what I am talking about. These people are so broken, and their dreams are so shattered. They have suffered so much pain and grief that they have become numb to the connection they have with the higher being. A strong connection with the higher being leads to a life of contentment. You know you have someone to turn to when things get tough, which is a good feeling to have.

The energy levels in a human body have an intricate relationship with their overall health. They are interdependent—if one part feels low or interrupted, it is bound to affect the other. Whenever you feel aggravated at the tiniest of things, you can diagnose your weakness and work on it. You'll know that you're not alone and whatever is happening to you is not something that cannot be treated.

It was an aha moment when I tried to control my world to be happy. I realized I was led by my ego and the emotional conditions of my past. One day, I had had enough of going in the wrong direction and being on the carousel of pain. I prayed to truly "let go and let God handle it." I just gave the universe my ego and control and begged the universe (or God) to show me the right way.

Now to let go of your ego and self-control is hard to do. I always felt I had the answers yet could not find the right path. It never occurred to me to let the universe or God just guild me. The promise that all will be more beautiful loving is really true. I remember the feeling really well, I just let the law of attraction and my power above have control of my life at that point. I focused really hard on what I truly wanted in my heart, and I let go. The next moment the miracles started to happen. It was amazing to go through this feeling like flowing down a river of glory instead of swimming upstream all the time. Since then, I trust in the energy of the universe or God. I use the law of attraction to set my intentions and watch for the clues to unfold. You have to have faith and trust all will be fine. You have to make sure you understand that you have to do the work, but the clues do come.

I just put one foot in front of the other each day and watched the miracles unfold before me. I have been letting the flow of the universe and God guide me ever since. It is utterly amazing to receive such a gift from Heaven.

Assignment

Today's activity is for you to evaluate the flow of energy within your chakras by yourself. Keep track of your behavior and analyze if the behavior that you exhibit is the reaction to any of your thoughts or any happenings in your life, both positive and negative. For example, if you feel irritated right now at this moment, work on finding the root of this negative energy. Once you diagnose what triggered these feelings, work on getting rid of them by self-care and treat it. See why you feel a certain way that you do. For example, see what helps you in clearing your chakras and helps your energy circulate better. Take notes of what exercises, or what sort of food intake, help you overcome a situation and finally rejuvenate your internal energy.

CHAPTER 4

HOW DOES IT WORK?

The Four Pillars of Energy:

Each of the four pillars is separate, yet all of them need to be understood together, and the importance of each needs to be worked on the same. Diet, exercise, emotions, and your higher power are the four pillars. They can all have higher and lower levels of energy vibrations. Each of these is important for raising your whole body and soul's vibrational energy to a point conducive to a healthy and happy life. The main gig is to understand how to integrate higher energy on each pillar. Vibrating higher will heal you at many levels along the way to achieve a more loving life.

Many great books about energy have taught me the levels of vibrations from 0 to 1000. We all live in a third-dimensional world today. This is living under the 200 level. Emotions and ego reactions mainly control life. David Hawkins in the book Power versus force, states 'the collective level of consciousness of all mankind remained at 190 for many centuries and only jumped to our current level of 207 with in the last decade'. This is out of the ego and emotional states of being and towards a more loving, healing world. All emotional states have a lower level of energy and cause harm to our bodies in one way or another.

Power Versus Force is a great book to understand VE levels. Today, we are starting to raise above the 200-level mark of vibrations. This is a level of healing and a point where the ego is no longer controlling your life. I want to help you achieve this state of being. We can achieve many greater energy vibrations, but today let us start with a pure state of healing and movement out of ego control. It is amazing to go through a day with no lower-level emotional state negativity bringing you down and getting in the way. Feeling the body healthy and energetic comes along with vibrating higher as well.

What is energy? How does it impact our existence and that of those around us? Literally, everything is energy in one form or another. As discussed earlier, it is the fundamental source of our being. How do we achieve serendipity through life? Wouldn't it be beautiful to feel serene and directed towards what we dream of becoming in life? When we dig deeper to understand the power of energy, we give ourselves the chance to be tuned in with synchronicity with the universe. Of course, *energy* is the key.

But How Do We Create It for Ourselves?

We dig deeper and understand the reliable sources are pillars of energy we have achieved so far: diet, exercise, emotions, and our higher power. We have the power within ourselves to create the miracles we could only imagine. The higher power is a higher vibration. To enhance the four pillars, we must understand the link between them and complement them in a more fulfilling way of life. The first pillar is the diet. Now, what do we mean by diet? It is not just the careful intake of food items we consume. It revolves around all that we are to consume daily. It is also the content we go through on social media or the books we read to feed our intellectual appetite. We apply the forms of meditation in our routines, be it religious or not, and last but not least, the type of food we take and the amount. Some food items have a higher amount of salts and sugars. These influence our blood pressure and cholesterol levels. I am more interested in the higher energy pure foods that are alkaline, not acidic. We will discuss those further in the later chapters. It is important to be selective with such food items. It is also important to understand that a good alkaline diet is crucial to a healthier body. Further, too much or too little of anything, or not taking in the right diet' can make you unhealthy.

Similarly, the reading and the educational content we feed our minds with can impact our intellectual well-being. Newton's Third Law of Motion suggests that *every action has an opposite and equal reaction.* You watch a horror movie, and the next thing you see is that you find yourself witnessing poltergeists in your bedroom, although it is never the case. Our mind plays tricks on us, and we must be careful with what we conceive. The Law of attraction can occur through a psychological chain of thoughts or ideas we place the most attention toward.

With the diet revolving around intellectual and nutritional intakes, spirituality plays the most crucial role. If you have attained a spiritual balance in life, you will most likely gain an emotional balance. What does it mean to be *spiritual?* The meaning may vary according to life experiences. To be fully inclined towards the mind, body, and soul in a manner that your vibration is in the right direction, you may be on the path to embracing spirituality. You are empathetic to what may lie ahead and beyond yourself.

You Are Not A Physical Form, But the Soul You Embody.

High Vibration You can perceive beyond logic. Hence, your steps to a spiritual path have taken place before you have acknowledged the same. When is spirituality most effective? The answer, when it is backed up by exercise. Exercise is the repetitive movement of your physiology. Be it through a gym routine, yoga, dance, or a sport. If you stay in motion that creates harmony for your physical well-being, you are likely to be spiritually and physically vibrational. You achieve clarity in the sense of fitness and concentration, and once you can do so, you will have more command over what comes your way.

With diet and exercise acting as the key pillars that add value to our physical well-being, emotional stability soon follows. However, a dynamic equilibrium does not refer to being- down or suppressing emotions. It is the act of being vulnerable in the right manner. You channel your negative emotions intelligently. You learn to acknowledge lower energy levels that are hurting you and do not let them affect your wellbeing. Think of your body as a processor or a machine that takes the raw emotion you feel and turns it into a sensation that allows you to create better situations for yourself. *A little patience can go a long way.* Being a human with high levels of emotions can often be seen as a flaw, but the more you can 'feel,' the closer you are to 'being.'

Each emotion has a vibrational energy level. You can be at an emotional level so low that it is close to death. I have been taught that 0 to 200 is where all negative emotional behavior vibrates. We need to understand our emotions and learn to raise ourselves above 200, i.e., courage. It is then that we can self-heal. I will go into detail later.

How do you manage to maintain your ego and not let it hurt you or those around you? Do you wish to use your defense mechanisms in a manner that they do not offend anyone? Well, empathy is a tool that allows you to do so.

"You can only understand people if you feel them in yourself." – John Steinbeck

Empathy is a skill that allows you to be emotionally intelligent and understanding towards those around you. You come across a heated encounter or a debate you do not wish to agree with. You may even be right and logical. Learning to understand where your emotions came from is the first step to freedom. Emotions have given us the strength to get past bad times and warn us before difficult situations arise. The key is to learn from them is not to let them control you in a harmful way.

We go through every day having to face other people and their emotional state. The key is how do we handle it to protect ourselves from any negative effects on our wellbeing. The key is to raise our vibrational energy field. The higher your energy field, the less low ego-based negative energy can affect you. The only way to be affected is to be at the same energy level they are feeling. If you are happy strong and understand how we rob each other's energy, then you will be ready to put up your bubble or field of energy around you to protect you from any energy robbing. It works amazingly to see a teenager try their hardest to rattle your emotions, and you do not get attached to their game. It is quite amusing to watch. They will go in melt down when they can get to you to play you for something. I mentioned creating a bubble around your aura. There is a way to protect yourself from others. You visualize a thick wall of gold around your aura field and body. This helps reflect the ability of others to be able to attach to you. You can give them loving energy to help them feel better. Giving free love to another is always good. And when an emotion comes into play on your emotions, you can sit back, take a moment to review the feeling or fear or hurt, and then react calmly.

We will learn to understand each emotion is a helper to guild us through a process. Some of our experiences have been harmful in the past, and we need to heal them and let them go. To heal, you need to release all your past emotional harms and fears. You do not let yourself connect to their energy power play. You can still engage in a conversation and not let your energy be sucked dry. The ego was a way to guide us through life, not to control our life reactively. The idea is to have great emotions, good and painful still, and still live a happy high vibrational energy life. In other words, learn how to let your emotions guild you, not control you.

Your higher power is your spirituality. It is the connection we all need to this earth and universe and all souls. When we can feel like a part of all life, we develop a sense of total oneness. Activities such as meditation, praying, long meditational hikes, and so many others can help ground oneself and achieve balance and learn to let go. This process will give you the calmness to ask the universe or God to guild you and help bring on the miracles you need.

Once we can master the four pillars: diet, exercise, emotions, and higher power, we are set free from the dilemma we would create for ourselves between *living or existing*. I was at the same spot when I began my journey towards becoming more enlightened in understanding my purpose and how to live my life to the fullest. Life is way too short for us all just to *exist*. We all want to make a mark, and if we can learn to channel our energy in ways that liberate us from the world's unnecessary drama, we will indeed be able to celebrate our cause in this life.

I Discovered More And More With Time

I experienced low levels of energy with the ailment that fate brought. With the spiritual and conscious exploration, I came across to add to my living, I wanted to learn about myself. I discovered more and more with time. It felt like 'happiness' was the main aim for an extended amount of time and that it was what I should be chasing midway to being successful. But the more I pursued this subjective term 'happiness,' the more adrift I became. What is happiness? I pondered, and I pushed on with whatever learnings I adopted along the way. But what became clear was the anxiety that chasing happiness brought into my life; it only caused a deeper hole and more yearning. I have let my emotions and past life experiences block my ability to feel free and happy. I lived through one painful experience to the next. I had achieved many degrees of happiness and success, yet I could not find the real joy I was genuinely searching for. I knew it was inside me but had no idea how to access it.

At that point in time, it hit me. I wondered, is that all there was? This question led to more questions. And this was not in a sanely inquisitive manner. I began to wonder how to get to or achieve this peaceful law of attraction state of being. I was grateful for my life and all that it had given me, but I had a deep longing to find the answer to living happily. How would I find my soul and connect to all others? I have always had a longing to help and heal folks when I could.

I search my whole life for answers to achieving a higher spiritual life and vibrational state. I felt it from birth and knew I had a purpose that included more than just living. I had a deep need to search for ways to heal myself and the world around me throughout my life. Through reading and studying metaphysics and meditation, and spiritual guidance, I found the answer was all about energy vibrations and living in the moment. I learned how to let my soul guild me. I found we start raising our vibrational energy in all four pillars, diet, exercise, emotions, and higher power.

You Must Truly Die to Become Fully Alive

When I came to know of my cancer, I witnessed low vibration and energy levels, which made me doubtfully question everything. I wasn't prepared for any of it. There was so much I wanted to do in life. There were places to go to—people to meet. I wanted a guiding light to get me through. Today, I always get energized in any state of hurt and fear and push my way through it with strength and determination. Cancer just made me stronger than I expected. It gave me the power to change my life in every way, to live better in this world. That meant diet and exercise needed to improve. It also meant the people that were harming me or had toxic traits required to go. I needed to change my job to a happier, more fulfilling one and mostly stay very close to my higher power to guide me.

I learned about holistic healing in immense depth. I went to the University of Metaphysics and read every book I could find there to learn about healing our bodies. All this came together with an understanding that it is all about our bodies' vibrational energy. We, in society, had lost this understanding a long time ago. Even though now my cancer is gone, my world is amazing and filled with miracles happening daily. Each day I give gratitude for all I have been blessed with. I don't live in the past, nor do I live in the future. I live with great love for today. I stay focused on what is important, and with this tunnel vision, it comes to me. It is utterly amazing.

I have had the pleasure in my life to get to know special people that have overcome the most daunting odds with utmost grace. They all have done this with determination, internal strength, and mostly a lot of personal healing. A male friend close to me was run over by a car. He was dragged 100 feet down the street in the wake of the impact.

His body was like a pretzel that was crushed, and he had TBI on the right side of his brain. He ended up in a coma for a long time. I spent many months trying to find him the right kind of help. I also made sure he was not taken advantage of by the medical world. He is a holistic mountain man and never wanted any drugs or bad science from the medical world. It was extremely hard to keep the medical establishment away and from harming him more. The harm I am referring to here includes over-medicating, unnecessary surgeries, bad care, etc.

I pushed hard to let him heal himself. He was into kundalini energy and self-healing. He spent many months working with his energy power and visualizing his body healing. Six months later, he was able to walk again, two years later, his brain was back better than ever, and today he is out living in the mountains – once again making the most of his life and truly thriving. The most amazing part: he did not have any surgeries and very little medication. All this was done by healing energy.

Another male chiropractor friend of mine had cancer of the colon. He, of course, is very holistic and did not want any chemicals, drugs, or standard harmful cancer treatment. He elected to have surgery then heal himself. Today he is still cancer-free. The amazing part is when they cut out cancer, they severed all nerves to his private parts. Normally that would mean no more sex. He spent two years visualizing the nerves regenerating and began getting sensation back. Today he can make love again. In the medical world, they said such healing would be completely impossible. All this was done by visualizing meditation and determination.

Two other ladies, I knew both had severe drug and alcohol problems and lost everything. This included their husband, their kids, and worst of all, all respect for themselves. I chose to help them when they were at that point of life or death. They chose to live, and I took them to get help. It did not come easy, but in time they found the strength to want to live. I refused to just let them die. Today both have a great high vibrational life. They have their kids back and live life with gratitude.

All these people have one thing in common. They overcame amazing odds, drew strength inside themselves, and now give back to help others. I have seen so many miracles in my life. I have lived miracles in my own life. I will say that having access to miracles is truly available for everyone. You do have to understand it takes faith, hard work, self-healing in all pillars, and manifesting your dreams through meditation.

Ego & Emotion

It is not easy to understand the damage ego and negative emotions can cause in our lives. It takes a lot of bravery to self-assess and analyze how we are reacting through our thought-process. Negative emotions can take a toll on our mental health, as well as our physical well-being. Research says that people that develop a psychosomatic mindset are more likely to be diagnosed with cancer and undesirable ailments. It becomes a vicious cycle; we start to attract unwanted events through short temper and egoistic barriers. We hold back from making the best of what life offers to us. We do not churn our emotions into creation. There are so many ways to make art. We can transform all the negative emotions we're suppressing in a positive manner that brings us peace. You can channel it through exercise or curate it creatively.

As done with balancing negative emotions, it is also advisable to balance your ego. Your defense mechanism can often boost ego conflicts in a manner that makes life difficult for you to get by. When we become open to expressing and giving from our soul, we do it unconditionally. This becomes liberating for us. But if you operate through ego, you become limited in your scope to reach out and express. Communication often becomes judgmental, narrowing down your reasons to fully take in the experience of giving and loving. You do things due to personal reasons. It is not the exchange of vital human expression but just a logical trade. Even though a lot of do's and don'ts are created in the world of professionalism, they are designed to limit one. In many ways, a lot of professional norms can make one perform with the ego. Which at times may not be wrong, but one must understand what ego-centric methods to alleviate in your personal life.

With ego-centric methods, your way of looking at life and love is very distinctive compared to soul-centric ways. There is always scarcity in terms of creativity. You are more about knowing than experiencing. You withhold more as opposed to be open. Your self-sabotage and impose it upon yourself to be logical, especially in terms of bad experiences. Thus, you limit yourself from taking chances or giving chances.

With the culmination of the four pillars of energy persistently carried out, you will find yourself at a more emotionally stable place. You will not only be more spiritually vibrational, but you will also have more command over the kind of 'diet' you should be consuming. It may come as a tardy process in which you may have to be selective about many personal and professional factors, but with time the good it will bring for you will only be explored as you keep it up. You are not alone on this journey; I am here for you. Think of it as we are walking through this insightful path together. Every day is a new day. Each second is another chance for you to gift to yourself.

The Fruits of a Positive Mindset

Let us discover the strength a positive mindset or meditation can do for you. This is one easy way to ground yourself and feel your peacefulness. I will walk you through an exercise that you can perform when your ego or temper shoots. You can create a space for yourself to walk to. Allow me to make a journey for you to always come back to in your favorite ways. Sit up, loosen your shoulders, and close your eyes. Take your right hand and slowly close your index finger with your thumb as you imagine your favorite memory. Create a vivid visual of scenery in your mind. Think about the sounds, the colors, the smells as closely as you can. Let your mind take you back to memory lane. While you become closer to the scene, close your finger and thumb tighter. You have the memory right between your fingertips. Let the sensations kick in. Let them elevate you. Do not hold back from smiling. Do it as much as you can and live within that moment. Stay there as long as you need to. Once you are ready to come back, slowly, and gradually release your fingers. You have just meditated to a memory that brings you ultimate bliss. You have been able to experience it fully within your body. Witness how your surroundings seem better than the moment when you had your eyes closed? Yes, you were able to time-travel. You now have the power.

The wonders mindfulness can perform are genuinely remarkable. You can snap out of negative emotion and step into a positive space that does you better. You can save yourself from diving into misery. But what I would request you to do, is be patient with the process. Mindfulness is not something you achieve overnight. However, the fruits start to greet you more and more as you dive deeper into meditation persistently. The more you practice and instill a calm mindset within yourself, the better off you are. You are not only able to represent yourself as a saner and wiser individual, but a humble one. After all, such heated debates can be very exhausting. Why act like a fool and waste your energy? You have so much to achieve in life. A lot of beautiful moments await you. With the thought-process you've been working on now, you're already on your ladder to spiritual success.

Every minute that you are now spending has more meaning. You are now tuned into your mind, body, and soul. Your vibration is your strength. With the accomplishment of higher vibrations, you are empathetic. You are inspiring to those around you. You are more likely to attract greatness. You are a miracle in the making.

CHAPTER 5

THE DIET

Why Is Healthy Lifestyle Important?

We all want to live a long and healthy life. We want to be the best version of ourselves, and it often seems so hard to do so with the world pacing so fast. Let me tell you this, the four pillars may only be challenging to begin with, but once they become a part of your lifestyle, you will have a better grasp at living a healthier life. You will see the miracles of health unfold. However, it will help more if you become more disciplined with your diet. After all, it is the most vital tool that impacts your vibration. The more command you have with your diet, the higher your vibrational energy would be.

A healthy diet will not just keep you fit and physically sound, but it will churn your existence towards manifesting all you have been waiting to attract in life. The healthier we are, the more fluent our potential is to be successful. To achieve all our dreams and objectives, we need to live a long and healthy life. Death and ailments are inevitable. They are prewritten by fate, but with a positive mindset encapsulating the four pillars, I assure you of a beautiful life. I will walk you through a tested diet plan which will help you experience a remarkable elevation in your vibration once you are on board with the suggested diets.

You Ever Wondered How Aging Occurs?

No one wants to grow old. We all want to stay fresh and active. In other words, we all want to remain young. It is not an impossible phenomenon, but let me tell you something, aging is just as beautiful and natural as the need to stay young and active. It is a beautiful process, and you must not fear it. Do not step into any complexes that get triggered through aging or growing older. It is the most incredible thing to happen, but what you can do is to accept that it is bound to happen and cherish what you have in store. That's right. I'm talking about making the best of what you have. Time and health. Let both be by your side by being in their side.

Let us discuss how aging occurs. Human bodies are just not built for extreme aging. The average capacity of the age of humans can have ninety years. But what does aging mean? And how does it counteract our bodies' efforts to stay alive? We can know intuitively what it means to age. For some, it means growing up, and for others, growing old. Yet finding a simple scientific definition of aging is a challenge. We can say aging begins when the interaction processes like water and sunlight cause toxins in our diets, causing the change in cells and molecule's functions and structure. Those changes, in turn, drive towards decline and subsequently add to the failure of the organism. The exact mechanism of aging can poorly be misunderstood. But recently, scientists have identified a physiological set of traits ranging from genetic changes to alterations in a cell's regenerative ability, which plays a particular role.

The Impact of Aging on Our Immune Systems

Our immune systems get damaged over time from reacting to short-term problems like inflammation. Our bodies levels down; for example, we lose the ability to hear as teenagers being exposed to loud music, our cognitive abilities peak in our mid-twenties. So, by the time we hit fifty, changes become increasingly noticeable. The risk factors that come along may lead to severe chronic diseases. There is a lot of unnecessary consumption we take in our daily lives, which may decrease our overall system level of vigor.

Nonetheless, do you know how easy it is to manage all these factors? The answer is the four pillars. We begin with diet, and then we move onto the other three step by step. We begin with a diet because we need to flush out and rid away all our system has been carrying for ages. We need to look at it as a transformation that will take place step by step. It's like reincarnation or miraculous rejuvenation happening to your system. Whatever you feed it with, that is how it will respond.

How Does Diet & Exercise Play a Crucial Role?

As discussed in earlier chapters, your diet is not just the daily intake of food. It is what and how you consume it. It revolves around our overall routine. Finding the right diet, the proper exercise that compliments your diet may take time, and a specific procedure. Considering that everyone's immune system performs differently, certain practices may be needed to adapt to a healthy diet and routine. When we take up any diet plan, exercise goes along the way. We must not forget the benefits it adds to our fitness and health objectives.

When we move, our entire physiology changes. It shifts from the state of mind and body into a progression that may elevate us physically and spiritually. Our brain is more active and focused. The negative energy flows out and channels productively. However, there should be a gradual increase in workout routines that add meditation to it. Through this, you can relax the muscles that have been stretched and worked heavily on. While you are at it, pat yourself on the back. Embrace the progression you are making and aid it to flow through. We now understand the importance of exercise and diet. It does not help us reverse aging but gives us vitality that allows living life to its fullest.

What Really Works:

Do you often feel uneasy after eating some food products? Kind of like a burning sensation or nausea that makes you feel lethargic? Foods with acidity can cause such feelings. It is rare to admit that the food items we are consuming can play such a role. It is not just the way our bodies react to food consumption but also our overall emotional well-being. Our moods, the diseases we encounter, the way we appear, the main factor is our diet. Most of you may already know the benefits and drawbacks of acidic and alkaline foods. If you do not, there is nothing to worry about. I am here to walk you through.

When we speak of diets and routines, we must not ignore the causes and effects of acidic foods and alkaline. You may compare it to fire. When things burn, they leave an ash residue; both have a chemical reaction that breaks down-solid mass. However, this process takes place gradually. Metabolic waste can be referred to as alkaline, acidic, or neutral fats. The alkaline diet is also known as the acid-alkaline ash diet. Its main aim is to alter the value of your pH level. We will also shed light on why having a balanced pH level is crucial. Your metabolism allows food to be converted into energy. Everything can become energy, and you can transfer vibrations.

One cannot understand the results of a particular practice or attempt unless and until it's performed consistently. There were times when I heard about holistic healing and higher vibrations before my cancer hit me, but I could not understand its effectiveness there and then. I had to try it myself to see if it works or not. These days it is hard to find something we want to stick with. We need to know what will work and not. Just like that, I also wanted to cherish myself. I deserved to take on life and make the best out of it. Time is a mere illusion. It limits us from creating the miracles we genuinely wish to. Yet the best way to go about time is to become its friend. Neither fear it nor try to control it. Take it easy with yourself, just one step at a time with absolute determination. That is when you see the effectiveness of a particular aspect. With your diet, you need the same approach.

Interesting, isn't it? I thought so too. When I formed these four pillars, mainly diet fundamentals, I knew beyond my daily consumption. What has worked and not? I could explore the wonders of knowledge that would not just allow me to alter my ways, but it gave meaning to whatever I would consume. If you eat foods that give you more acidic waste, you are more likely to produce alkaline ash. According to the acid-ash hypothesis, acidic ash makes you vulnerable to illness and disease, whereas alkaline ash is considered protective. If you consume more alkaline foods, you would be able to alkalize your body and enhance your health.

When I regularly performed these habits, I felt tuned into life and more in charge of my system, and I know you can too. The food components that leave acidic ash have proteins, phosphate, and sulfur, while alkaline features include calcium, magnesium, and potassium. You can monitor your diet plan accordingly. With the alkaline diet, you may have a healthier lifestyle and a lighter yet cooperative immune system. It will take time and effort. Trust me, all outstanding achievements in life require time.

The Wonderous Alkaline Foods For Your Diet

Alkaline Foods			
Vegetables	Summer squash	**Grains, Cereals**	**Diary & Meat**
Artichokes	Sweet Potatoes	**& Breads**	None
Asparagus (tips)	Swiss chard	Amaranth	
Bamboo Shoots	Tomatoes	Buckwheat	**Condiments &**
Broccoli	Turnips	Kamut	**Spices**
Beetroots	Watercress	Millet	(Unfermented Soy)
Bell Peppers	Wheat grass	Quinoa	Almond Butter
Brussels Sprouts	Wild Greens	Spelt	Bee Pollen
Cabbages	Zucchini	Sprouted Breads	Bragg Aminos
Carrots		Sprouted Tortillas	Chili Pepper
Cauliflowers	**Fruits**	Yeast-Free	Cinnamon
Celery	Avocados	Breads	Curry Powders
Chard	Grapefruits		Ginger
Chayote	Lemons	**Sweets &**	Guacamole (fresh
Chicory	Limes	**Desserts**	made)
Chives	Tomatoes	None	Herbs (all)
Collard Greens			Houmous
Cucumbers	**Oils & Fats**	**Beans &**	Lemon Juice
Dandelions	Avocado Oil	**Legumes**	Lime Juice
Dills	Coconut Oil	All moderately	Sea Salt
Dulce	Flax Oil	acidic	
Eggplant	Hemp Seed Oil		**Oriental**
Endives	Olive Oil	**Nuts & Seeds**	**Vegetables**
Garlic	Safflower Oil	Almond Butter	Daikon
Green Beans	Sesame Oil	Almonds	Dandelion Root
Green Olives		Carraway Seeds	Kombu
Green Peas	**Grasses &**	Cumin Seeds	Maitake
Greens (leafy)	**Sprouts**	Fennel Seeds	Nori
Horseradishes	Alfalfa	Hemp Seeds	Reishi
Jerusalem	Alfalfa Sprouts	Pumpkin Seeds	Sea Vegetables
Artichokes	Amaranth Sprouts	Sesame Seeds	Shitake
Kale	Barley Grass	Sunflower Seeds	Umeboshi
Kelp	Broccoli Sprouts		Wakame
Leeks	Dog Grass	**Drinks**	
Lettuces	Fenugreek	Alkaline Water	
Mustard Greens	Sprouts	Barley Grass	
Okra	Kamut Grass	Huide	
Onions	Kamut Sprouts	Coconut Water	
Oyster plants	Lemon Grass	Fresh Lemon &	
Parsley	Millet Sprouts	Lime Water	
Parsnips	Mung Bean	Fresh Veg Juices	
Peas (fresh)	Sprouts	Green Drinks	
Peppers	Oat Grass	Green Tea	
Radishes	Quinoa Sprouts	Herbal Tea	
Rutabagas	Shave Grass	Wheat Grass	
Sea Veggies	Spelt Sprouts	Juice	
Spinach	Wheat Grass	Udo's Choice	
Sprouts (all)		Beyond Greens	

What Are the Effects of Acidic Foods On Your Energy?

Have you ever noticed how your energy levels randomly fluctuate throughout the day? It is mostly because of high levels of sugars and salts. These levels take away a lot of health, which I will further elaborate upon. Levels of acidity can seriously impact your vibrational energy. You may want to monitor your intake that creates acidity. These elements do not just cause unhealthy factors but make you age more while lowering your vibration. Lower vibrations can have a massive effect on your overall well-being. So, I would advise you to go along with a diet plan that has a balance of Alkaline. I could tell you my personal story of how I was able to balance my pH levels. I remember it was done through the intake of a detailed diet plan. Do not be so surprised; there were people in my life that put in a lot of work to achieve higher vibrations through these steps that I will tell you of.

I focused on taking foods that had a balance of Alkaline and alkaline acidity. It did take time to monitor and understand what would suit my body. With the help of various detox routines, the removal of many acidic foods became easier. I have gone around various detox programs, which I will shed light upon later, that helped me heal significantly. The great learning, I achieved through holistic healing is that the cure lies within us. With every disease that comes your way, the healing is within it. I vividly recall when my cancer had begun, and I was at rock bottom. Like you, there were many food products included in my diet that I would consume without thinking twice. We are not always aware of the damages happening within us until something knocks on our door in the shape of an ailment.

All I wanted to do was establish my way up. I was only able to do so with sheer determination and hard work. I manifested miracles within myself that raised my energy to a level where I could attract more incredible healing. It all made me realize that I was capable of so much more than my disease. Now we both know that achieving beyond your benchmark does not happen overnight. You must stay persistent and active. Every day was about making sure I took all the baby steps that added to a solid foundation. I have a gift for you; here is a diet plan you may want to know. I know these will balance your pH levels. I am following these tips along with you.

1. **Pick just natural, non-GMO nourishments.** You'll dodge pesticides, synthetic compounds, and different impurities that are corrosive creating.

2. **Eat soluble shaping nourishments.** Most greens are. Avocados, strawberries, and almonds are my top pick; however, every verdant green vegetable and each spice is on the rundown also.

3. **I have found seeds to be the embryo of all great nutrition.** The top 10 seeds are the most powerful ones you can eat. The amazing nutritional value of each raw seed is so valuable in your daily diet. I recommend making a mixture of all ten and have a scoop full each day in your salad, smoothie, fun mixed in your meal. The top seeds are chia, sesame, flax, hemp, black, grape, pomegranate, cumin, pumpkin, sunflower. Eat them raw or grind them up to digest better.

4. **Try less refined sugars, flours, and meats.** You ought to eat about 40-50 grams of protein daily.

5. **Work on suppers vigorously.** Blend a good balance of alkaline foods, so you have a perfect balance. A lot of color in all your meals. As I say, "no white anything in my diet."

6. **Most importantly, eat potassium-rich nourishments:** lemons, bananas, nectar, yams, or crude, standard yogurt.

7. **Squeeze a large portion of a lemon and blend into an 8 oz. glass of warm water to free your assemblage of overabundance acids and make a primary state.** Drinking this first thing flushes your core and sets you up for the day.

8. **Drink loads of water every day.** It is the ideal approach to guarantee your structure is highly functional. Drinking water causes move the loss to where it tends to be canceled. Drink 7-8 glasses per day.

9. **I also love a complete meal replacement drink to get me alkaline and balance each morning.** It is really hard to eat enough food with all its nutrition these days. Farming has

taken out a lot of the nutritional value in food grown today. I believe a great, well-balanced organic meal with proteins and lots of fruit and vegetables is key. It will also get you rocking with energy day.

My friend, whom I had mentioned in earlier chapters, who struggled with drinking and drug abuse, also opted for detox programs that complemented the four pillars. I know it wasn't easy for her to do so, but her willpower and ascertainment enabled her to master her vibration. Not only was she able to come out of the habit of drinking and drug abuse, but she was also able to work towards her life aims more insistently. Until you step into the holistic approach toward life, then you will know why I became so gratified with this lifestyle.

Why Is It Essential to Avoid Such Foods?

If you aim to stay healthy and youthful, you will have to monitor your entire system and see how everything works for you. If you wish to maintain a healthy lifestyle, you must pay attention to the foods you intake, such as the white foods and the damages it causes to your system. The bleaching agent added to white foods like flour and sugar takes away the actual value it can add to your diet. It causes inflammation in your gut, which can lead to unpleasant energy levels. With skin, it causes acne, which can also be a problematic situation to have. Apart from dermatological issues, bleached sugars can also cause colon cancer and add to cardiovascular problems. These can halt our ambition to live a longer and healthier life. I know this may seem odd to hear, but I had to rid away many sugar agents from my diet to come at the vibration I am today.

Similarly, the white flour is also deprived of iron; thus, you can interact with gluten issues. They cause fattening. The actual fiber you need for a sound digestive system required for you to maintain a healthy and balanced diet is counteracted with problems that halt your vibration. They cause swelling and acidity within our system, making it more challenging to be functional and active. If you wish to live a longer and more wholesome life, you may avoid such foods that include acidity. I know that as you work on doing so, you will be able to manage the negative effect that comes your way. Even though sicknesses are an inevitable phenomenon, but with an alkaline diet, you will be more secure from disease development. I am telling you, this works like a magic spell.

The Role of Nutrition

We often confuse fruit sugar and white sugar and tend to decrease our intake of fruits, thinking that it will cause the same effect. Being diabetic might be an issue, but if you measure the drawbacks of bleached sugar or fruit sugar, you will understand the adverse effects of fruit sugar are way lower than bleached sugar. They also add more vitality to your years and reduce the risk of your diseases.

Here's a fact; the optimal range for humans is 7.30-7.45 (slightly acidic). But you see, there is a problem—our stomachs may demand acid to break down food, but acid helps bacteria, viruses, and fungi to reproduce. If you feel like you are not alkaline enough, you can work towards detox programs and diet plans that help your immune system.

There are many detox programs we can adapt to, and each comes with a different diet. There are Detox programs that we can take help from to assist our systems. Nonetheless, it may help eliminate the excess of unrequired acid inducements in our immune system, causing our vibration to lower. With detox programs aiding our diet and lifestyles, we can balance our pH levels.

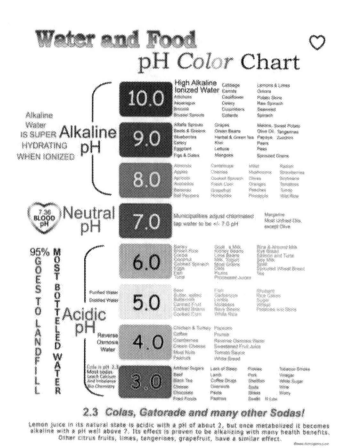

I recommend a good 30-day detox program to cleanse your visceral fat. This is the fat around your organs that holds onto a lot of toxins. Make sure you get your doctor's approval first.

I will tell you my alkaline cancer-fighting diet that has been amazing at keeping my body fit and healthy. It starts in the morning lemon water drink. Breakfast usually is a full meal replacement drink to balance my body to an alkaline balance. This gives me the energy to start my body off in a healing mode. Snacks are nuts, fruit, dark chocolate. Lunch is a very colorful salad with some protein—lots of water throughout the day and, of course, teas. Dinner is a likely combination of veggies, protein, and healthy carbs. Be as colorful as you can in your choice of food. I have a healthy supply of different vitamins and herds. And my 10 top seeds are added to everything raw.

When we walk through the holistic healing approach, which would help us accomplish a higher vibration, we learn the significance of the four pillars of energy. Every pillar has its implication. Diet plays a fundamental role; we learn how to eliminate toxins from our system and introduce ourselves to diet plans that rejuvenate our spirits and energy. Diet and detox go hand-in-hand with exercise. Now, I do not advise you on heavy workout routines with detox.

Once you accomplish the flow and benefits of a healthy lifestyle, you will start to feel higher vibrations that enable you to have a more welcoming aura. The aura you develop will add more meaning to your personality and manifest a lot more for you that paves a successful life direction. The more you have command over the four pillars, the better you will understand why so many people have opted to live this way. Here is a project for you to think about today. Look back at your diet and make a list of what your normal diet has been. Be realistic and honest with yourself. Now write how you feel throughout your day and week. Do you feel a slump during the day? How do you handle the up and downs of the food you eat? Do you eat or drink to deal with emotions? Now start planning a great healthy meal plan to get you alkaline and feeling full of energy. Now start eating right and feel the massive difference in your vibrational energy.

CHAPTER 6

EXERCISE

Do you know what it is like to become fully tuned in to your heart, mind, soul, and body? Have you ever felt complete synchronicity with all that you are inclined to become? Each nerve, every bone in your system, and your entire blood flow cooperates with your brain in unison. It is a 'yes' from the heart to *you* as a whole. With complete mind, spirit, and intellect, you are *one*. You smile, and the smile is not an ordinary one; it is genuine because your body is also smiling. It is not involuntary or imposed but created and felt profound. It is the purest form of expression from your *aura* to the world around you. You are a beautiful *magnetic* force that everyone wants to experience. You are so close to *becoming* it. I assure you. Walk with me, hold my hand, and tell me; what has kept you from *experiencing* this ultimate form of *vitality*?

The Miracles Of Movement

I know there has been a lot you need to look after. It has not been an easy road at all. Life has become hard, and that, too, in many ways. It is demanding and requires us to always be on our toes. Many depend on us, and we have to mold our circumstances accordingly. Believe me when I tell you this—you have been doing a remarkable job. I know you have been getting up every day and doing your best to become one with your purpose. You *truly* are. Look at you now. Look at where you stand. Isn't it incredible? You have come so far. Sure, we have a lot more to accomplish and walkthrough. Instead, today, we will move. We will understand what it is like to be in motion—the miracles of movement and the gift we can give to ourselves by exercising regularly. You are beautifully performing the four pillars. I can already sense your vibration. It is a gift to us all. Don't you feel the difference? I am sure you do.

We always discuss that we need to exercise. It is fundamental to achieving a higher vibration. But, today, we will understand why it is the most vigorous gift we can give to our bodies. Tell me, how often do we dance, move, exercise, or be in motion? How often is it that when times are rough and days are heavy, we feel immobile physically? Quite very so. It is all right to experience pain, stress, and lethargy. We all are humans, and these are familiar sensations to come across. What is the secret to transforming it? How do we raise our vibration? How do we make life look like art and appreciate it as it deserves to be? The obvious answer is through exercise. It is the act of being in motion or movement.

As Our Physiology Changes, Our Immune System Gets Better

We are so fortunate with the bodies we have. The kind of flexibility we can create through the practice of physical exercise is remarkable. You will be surprised by the impact it has on our overall well-being. We can take all the unwanted energy we feel and churn it into a positive, welcoming one by exercising. Have you ever wondered why changing our physiology is so important? Why do you think all the athletes, celebrities, and healthy people advise us to exercise regularly? As our physiology changes, our immune system gets better. We need to have better and faster metabolisms. When we exercise periodically while incorporating the diets I have mentioned in the previous chapters, we witness a healthier, lighter lifestyle that impacts our overall wellbeing. We do not just become more nutritious, but we become happier. You will find exercise as a sign of every healing routine, be it psychological, physical, or even spiritual. Exercise is the sacred act of being in motion. To function, you need to exercise. If we do not exercise, we can become a victim of countless diseases, including obesity. These not only harm our vibration but bring a halt to our concentration. It alleviates us from moving further ahead productively and in synchronicity.

Do you ever think why most psychologists advise exercise to the people who are suffering from depression? Do you know why they do it? The benefits are countless. Exercise not just helps maintain a healthy metabolism, but it keeps the blood flow better. It enables your heart to pump faster, and, for the moments it does, your heart can appreciate life more. It is a beautiful feeling. Do you know when you dance or play your favorite sport, you're experiencing the adrenaline your body craves? It sends signals to your brain, which allows you to feel alive. This is when the happy chemicals are released, and your brain and body then flush out depression or anxiety.

Without changing our physiology, it is difficult for us to recover or heal from mental illnesses. It will help if exercise can be a part of our routine. Training will enable you to become saner and give you a better sleeping cycle that will also enhance your memory and brainpower. This means you will be more focused and have higher energy. It is so essential for us to have a healthy sleeping schedule. A healthy sleeping pattern is like oxygen to our mind and body.

We really cannot rely upon a diet or other fundamentals of vibration when we do not exercise. Let me tell you what happens when you exercise. As your heart rate increases, your blood flow is instantly amplified that impacts your brain. This way, your brain receives more oxygen and nutrients.

Cognitive Health Through Exercise

The brain then develops proteins that are required to recover from many psychological and physiological illnesses. Studies say people who exercise regularly tend to be happier than those who do not. There were times when I had not taken it seriously either. But when I developed the four pillars and understood that high vibration requires exercise, I had to keep it an active part of my routine. How do we feel happier because of movement? The answer is simple. Your body releases chemicals like dopamine and endorphins in your brain, instantly moving you to a better mood. If you look at all the renowned athletes, dancers, celebrities, and healers, they all exercise one way or another. They keep a healthy diet that complements their fitness routines. My world has always been all about connecting to the earth in as many ways as possible. Exercise has been a vital source of it.

I have been very fortunate to experience our planet's greatest treasures. As I see it, the more open we become towards receiving these gifts given to us by God, the more we come to appreciate life. It was always a variety of ways since I like to push myself further and welcome whatever may come my way. Sometimes it would be a hike in the woods or a walk in the park. Sometimes it would be kayaking because it has a unique tranquility to it. Bicycling, swimming, yoga—anything that connects you to the earth has fantastic healing properties. Be open to receiving the best from this beautiful planet and, step by step, explore what works for you. The world gives us oxygen, and we give it carbon dioxide back. The balance of life is perfect. We just need to understand it. It is right in front of us each day.

The wonderments of exercise can be found within our everyday lives. You feel bad, physically, or emotionally; you take a walk, a run, or go for a bike ride in the park amongst nature. You can make your haven, and that can be the time you exercise. Like I always say, if something is keeping you stuck, bring in movement. I climb mountains since I live in Colorado. I still feel amazing after a good connection to nature and some H2O. As nature and exercise are essential sources for us to have a higher vibration and live better lives, water intake is crucial with all our workout routines. We need to stay constantly hydrated. It keeps our system and immunity flushed and rejuvenated. If we focus on it as a healer and a vital energy source, we will feel a remarkable change. Water is a magnificent gift from God. Did you also know that H2O can suck out negative energy from the air around you? We must not underestimate this beautiful gift of nature. God knows why we cannot survive without it. It just needs concentration and meditation, and we must drink it as if it is something sacred or even as a cure to so many illnesses. After all, whatever treatment or practice you begin needs determination and commitment. You intend for it, and it happens. The brain that meditates is a potent tool. When you do it to serve or heal your body, you will see how quickly you can adapt to a better and more beautiful lifestyle. We acknowledge that the more water we drink, the more toxins we flush out through our bodies.

Become Entirely In Sync Through The Four Pillars Of Energy

You can become more grounded and into the moment when your body is at peace. When you become entirely in sync through the four pillars of energy, you will manifest the most recreational moments that allow you to experience life to the fullest. When I moved to CO, I started hiking and biking. The fantastic high from connecting to the earth is so deep and peaceful. I give thanks each day I get to share time with all that the world has to offer. Gratitude also does wonders. The more we practice it, the more appreciative we become towards life. We develop a more flexible and humbler attitude towards life. We become more welcoming and open-minded. We can deal with tests and trials more smartly and humbly. Our way of responding to life's challenges transforms into a greeting method.

There are so many things we frequently do that can help us become healthier and flexible. It is all about the kind of attention you want to place on your movement throughout the day. I have found ways to exercise all day long, keeping in mind just specific exercises and use what I have near me like counters. Many stretches are used as a balance to do deep knee bends, leg lifts, and so much more. Use your imagination and create a workout throughout your day. You may use your grocery bags, do a few arm curls, or do lunges while you vacuum. How about a few stomach crunches while hanging on the sofa or office chair? These are just my suggestions. I am sure you may have many fun and creative ways to contribute to your physical and spiritual well-being throughout your routine. You can figure out so many ways to become one with your entire self. It is all about becoming more aware of the moment passing and how you choose to express gratitude towards yourself and life.

When you become focused on making the most of your routine through exercise, you will begin to understand how beautiful it feels to have a higher vibration. You will feel more active and youthful; activity decreases aging significantly. If we look at all the people in Asia, like the Chinese and Japanese, and how simplified they have made their routines, we will come to witness a lot of secrets to staying youthful, the intake of a high amount of H2O and an active practice throughout the entire day. I had a friend who had beautiful skin with a glow that never faded. She was so perfectly fit, and I had assumed her age to be relatively young. When I got to know the truth, I was surprised. Her secret was a high amount of water intake and that, too, lukewarm. Warm water helps your total immunity. If you are exercising and you keep a daily practice of drinking warm water, you will come to understand that our immunity is flushing out the unrequired toxins.

Similarly, I have seen some people older than I am who are so vibrant and healthy. They have a better command of aging because they regularly exercise. They do not have excuses. Instead, they make sure that each day life is their playground, and they play well. It would surprise me as well. How can one not miss a day of diet or exercise? How are they so prone to the fundamentals of energy? Will I be able to manifest a higher form of vibration as they have? Yes, and so will *you*. It is somewhat hard initially, but once you become accustomed to living life to the fullest, you will not want to live any other way.

The Healer

I once met a man who had become a Healer. He did not come from a comfortable past, nor did he practice the pillars before understanding their importance. He told me how he struggled with a negative mindset and lower vibration after a terrible car accident. He would suffer from a lack of concentration, which often drifted him from being successful at what he wanted to become. He had very unhealthy habits; he had started drinking excessively and was at a low point in life when he met a fellow he used to swim with back in college. He was a gold medalist when it came to swimming. His college fellow knew about meditation and healing, and he helped him get back on track by concentrating on swimming and meditation. That is when exercise came to play with meditation. By meditating and swimming regularly, he was able to gain strength and the mental capacity to overcome his bad habits. He sought the cure and the secrets to achieving your dream through exercise and meditation. These two sources were crucial to have more concentration. When he understood the secret of healing, he became a Healer and brought significance with his service. You can overcome anything you want in life. People have done it, and so have I. I know you are on your way to it too. Start your day more beautifully and actively, and witness how in-tune you can become with the earth.

By now, we have understood how to transform our negative energy into health through exercise. All the elements of nature can complement our fitness routines significantly if we give it the kind of attention it requires to amplify our vibration. Without exercise, we cannot live to our fullest. We really cannot enjoy the fruits of God given to us in the form of our physical self. It just requires training and an open mind that practices gratitude. Once you make it a habit to do so, you will experience the miracles you have been waiting to have. Keep walking through with me. You are doing an excellent job. Just some more steps left, and you can achieve all. I assure you.

Before we step out of the wonderments exercise and nature can bring for us, I have a task for you. I want you to become healthier and fit as you raise your vibration to the fullest. For this, you need to read your routine as a mentor. Be critical but know that we have the solutions to solve all our troubles. The cure lies within you; it always has and always will. Check yourself and see where you stand. Analyze your routine and understand how much you exercise, or if you even exercise at all. What are the things you can remove from your way that are causing your health to deteriorate? How can you be more flexible? What creative ways can you bring in more movement to your life and create a more beautiful sync with yourself?

Think about it all and come up with a routine for yourself. Make it a doable and enjoyable one that you feel you can stick with. I know you have the confidence to start, and I know you have the strength to keep up with it. You are to make miracles happen and enjoy a satisfying life. Your vibration deserves to rise in a manner you can manifest the best for yourself. It is your very right to do so. Love yourself and your body. Give it all the gifts it deserves. Observe life with more gratitude, and you witness how everything you had been waiting to have will come to you like a magnet.

CHAPTER 7

EGO: MIND, RELATIONSHIPS, AND SEX

The Psyche

The human psyche has been among the most mysteriously fascinating concepts the human mind itself can ever fathom. The ideology behind it suggests that we all are a product of the mind, the social norms, or the perceptions we adapt to, in addition to the behaviors we perform through the subconscious mind. Hence all the actions and reactions we deliver are a product of our psyche. The psyche comprises all that there is to be human, i.e., the soul, life, and breath. If we speak of all the psychological theories that define the human psyche, we will learn that the ego plays a crucial role. The ego allows us to form the concept of our 'self' and is an essential element of the cognitive process.

The term ego was originated in the early 19ᵗʰ century and directly meant the I. The 'I' can often lead to a stunt in our spiritual growth as the path to enlightenment requires us to look at internal and external progression differently. We need to tame the ego in ways that make us capable of transcending as human beings. When we think with the ego or conceive a specific aspect, we assume that we are logical – ego deceives us. We are limiting ourselves from pure human expression. We need the complete form of human expression, both to give it and to receive it.

Understanding the 'I' may help in understanding psychological disorders or how to cure them. Still, as far as our vibrational energy is considered, the ego can be very problematic. To understand how the ego can become problematic for our spiritual and intellectual growth, let me tell you the kind of problems it often creates for us. The biggest flaw that ego brings to our personality is that we assume that we are always right. No one is continuously right. We all are human beings that can often be misunderstood or be wrong. We are also conditioned to react to life's problems that face us by being conditioned throughout childhood and adulthood. We react and assume we have the answer due to our ego conditions. We then start to think that we are always right; by doing so, we become arrogant. We also become stubborn or controlling, and as we do that, we not only begin to live in this negative loop, but we also create a wall between ourselves and actual learning experiences. There are so many times that we suffer due to our ego.

We Suffer Due To Our Ego

Our ego is built around many lower vibrational energy emotions. They have strong emotional value to help deal with traumatic times. This development makes our conditional existence and builds our perception of the right way to live and react to life. In the long run, these conditioned emotions can do us harm. It can be done both in a physical and emotional reaction way of living. We all have the right to live life; however, our heart and path take us, but we also have to be careful that the ego-based emotions are not hurting us or holding us back from true growth. Fear and pain can stop us from living many great moments.

I did not understand how damaging the ego is until I started focusing on my healing and the four pillars. I need you to understand this from a second-person perspective as well as first. Because when you allow yourself to be in the shoes of another, you will realize their side of the story. Then, when you analyze yourself, you can understand how your immediate emotional reaction may not be the best thing to do.

Taking that deep breath and waiting to react and thinking about why you feel this way first before you emotionally react is way more useful. Use our emotions to guild us to think first and use this strong emotion as a guild to help us not hurt the other. If you do not do this, you will lose empathy. I will tell you why compassion is such an important tool.

There are so many negative emotions that come with being emotionally reactive that can damage our growth and especially our energy. God created us all as one. If we are not taking human expression's full experience, how will we learn to forgive ourselves and those around us? Remember that our conditioning from childhood has taught us how to stay safe from harm. We have established a strong value of emotions to guild us and keep us safe. They are meant to guild us, not control our lives. When strong low vibrational emotions control our happiness and health, then they are not helping us. They are holding us back from being truly happy.

To gain wisdom, we need to let go of the ego. It is not as hard as it seems. I have done this too. Higher vibrational energy life is learned by letting go of ego-based emotions. We are still living with our emotional makeup we have learned, but now we learn to use our ego as a helper and guild. The benefits of letting it go are far more than hanging on to it. I will explain in more detail.

The Levels Of Energy

I like to refer to David Hawkins's book "Power vs. Force. It has a great chart I will share to show you the vibrational energy levels of emotions. We want to be above 200 to live out of the ego and to a level of healing and peace. 0 to 200 are lower levels of energy that cause mental and physical harm to our body. The ego controls negative emotions in the lower vibrations. This is also in the 1st, 2nd, and 3rd dimensions of living. We want to live in the 4th dimension above 200 and free of letting harmful emotions control our lives.

The lowest level is 20, shame. Shame is humiliation close to death. You are miserable and want to be invisible. Very prone to physical illness.

Level 30 is guilt, which often goes with blame. Guilt is a symptom of victimhood and results in psychosomatic disease and suicidal behavior. Guilt provokes rage. Level 50 is apathy, which leads to despair and hopelessness. The world and future look bleak. This level needs external help to bring us out of helplessness. Very unhealthy and passive death is the outcome. Level 75 is grief and expresses regret, and the life view is tragic. This level is sadness, loss, dependency. Often is depression and sadness see a negative world all around them. Level 100 is fear and is anxiety or frightening. You live in a world of endless worrisome events. Fear becomes obsessive, and it limits the growth of our personality. It takes energy to rise above fear. Illnesses overgrow at this level. Level 125 is Desire, which is craving and disappointment. This helps us expand great effort to achieve goals and rewards. It is also a level of addiction because of the craving. Desire can help us move to a higher level too. Level 150 is anger which is hate. It is the aftermath of a situation causing resentment or frustration. Anger can lead to erosion effects on all areas of your life. Level 175 is pride, which is often demanding. You feel better than any of the lower levels, but it is defensive and vulnerable because it depends on external conditions.

Pride is fueled by the inflated ego and is vulnerable to attacks. The downside is arrogance and denial, which blocks growth. Now we all want to get to 200 and over to get out of the ego-based emotions and to a happier, healthier emotional level. 200 is courage and is the first level of power. Now life seems exciting, challenging, and stimulating, we are now coping with and effectively manage life opportunities. Obstacles that defeat people at the lower levels now act as a stimulant. We now give energy back to the earth. We help heal.

Level	Log	Emotion	Life View
Enlightenment	700 – 1000	Ineffable	Is
Peace	600	Bliss	Perfect
Joy	540	Serenity	Complete
Love	500	Reverence	Benign
Reason	400	Understanding	Meaningful
Acceptance	350	Forgiveness	Harmonious
Willingness	310	Optimism	Hopeful
Neutrality	250	Trust	Satisfactory
Courage	200	Affirmation	Feasible
Pride	175	Scorn	Demanding
Anger	150	Hate	Antagonistic
Desire	125	Craving	Disappointing
Fear	100	Anxiety	Frightening
Grief	75	Regret	Tragic
Apathy	50	Despair	Hopeless
Guilt	30	Blame	Evil
Shame	20	Humiliation	Miserable

Emotional Sabotage

Did you know that people can steal our energy through emotional sabotage? Emotional sabotage is when one is deeply connected with expecting from another, and this person maliciously harms your feelings attached to the matter at hand. They use your weak points against you and play the victim in a debate or time of disagreement. It can also lead to emotional breakdowns where you become disappointed and cannot understand how to help yourself or the other — people who are egoistic like to have a mindset that gives them power over your vulnerabilities. It all becomes about power play and manipulation. Such people are damaging to your energy.

The basic idea of emotional sabotage or I call it energy stealing, is when one steals energy from another person. We have been taught to steal energy from others through lower ego-based manipulation techniques. We all have a big energy field around us. For instance, when someone feels low on their energy field. Like a bad day at work or feels anger, grief, shame, they crave more energy. Subconsciously we have been trained to steal from each other to get more energy to feel better, a big power play. It is quite amazing to see someone steal the other's energy through negative manipulating techniques. We must understand that we can avoid this power play from others when we live in higher vibrational energy. Like a boss that is critical and spiteful and makes you feel horrible after an attack. Well, your higher energy reflects his power play to steal your energy. You are not affected, and most of the time, the other person will act better after because he did not get what he was used to getting. I would have other employees come to me and say, 'how did you deflate him so easily? And get him not to be so rude'. I say it is easy; do not get attached. You are taking the first steps to understand how lower vibrations can cause so much harm to our lives in so many ways. Now we can rise above this and truly live an amazing life.

Did you know that even you can be the one to carry these toxic traits? Understanding your flaws requires bravery. But you can only begin to apprehend yourself once you allow yourself the freedom of expression. You must learn to find your own mistakes before blaming anyone else. We all need to closely examine each vibrational energy level and see if we are dealing with some painful past experiences. I also will say we grow in layers like an onion—one layer at a time. So be patient to let the pains and fears come to the surface as they need healing. We can, at that time, learn to experience the pain again in a different way and breath through the emotion, and let it go. The idea is not to get involved with this emotional cycle from hell. Learn to understand the emotion and forgive ourselves and the other party, then give it to the universe.

It is an amazing relief to let a traumatic emotion go and heal from it. People who are egoistic and enjoy emotional sabotage tend not to apologize or be aware of their dangerous energy robbing. They become used to getting their way and function along as there can never be anything wrong with them. If you know everything, to begin with, portrays that you do not know anything at all. The universe has offered us so much; there are so many creations of God for which we have yet to deliver gratitude.

Similarly, when we limit ourselves from understanding the other and think with our ego, we restrict the other from reaching out to us. When we choose the ego, we create walls in our relationships. Those walls tend to make us paranoid and presumptive. This not only damages trust between two people but takes away the value you can add to the relationship. You become judgmental, and you think that whatever you are feeling is right. You do not give others the chance to express themselves to you, and you begin to fight instead of communicating. We get caught in our negative perceptions and lose sight of what we have and can create due to the poor perceptions we have developed.

All Emotions Have A Beginning, And We Have To Find The Beginning Point To Truly Heal It, And Let It Go

A good story to illustrate how easy our ego and emotions can damage a relationship or good moments is when my friend was visiting his son and girlfriend for a sabbatical time. She went with plans to stay for the winter. Great time to reflect and heal from the past. She was planning to get a place and a job, but her age made it difficult. She was staying at her sons for a few months, and Thanksgiving was coming up. She loves her son and girlfriend, but she could tell they needed their place back without mom hanging out. They gently asked her to find a place or go home soon. They wanted the holidays to themselves. My friend took this hard. She felt totally abandoned. She had nowhere to go that quickly. She said she went to the beach and cried for a few days. I guided her to tell her to let go and take this feeling of total abandonment, and let's find out where it started.

All emotions have a beginning, and we have to find the beginning point to heal it and let it go truly. We talked through the years of hurt, loss, and rejection that had affected her. As we went back through the years and let go of each part that she felt rejection and abandonment, she said she felt better. She finally reached the start of her fear. She grew up when hugging, holding, and showing too much love was to be wrong in raising a child. You were put in a crib and left to cry. She realized that she felt the first pain of abandonment when she would cry and cry. She said she remembers that when she stopped crying, her mother would come in and check on her and kiss her. She learned incredibly young just to be silent and don't make a lot of clatters.

This simple event at a young age affected her way of living her whole life. She realized this and asked the universe or God to take the pain away and heal this trauma. Now sitting by the beautiful ocean shore, a weight of a thousand pounds lifted off her body, and all felt beautiful and happy. It was not about her son and girlfriend's rejection. It was the past coming up to the surface very painfully while ready to heal. The miracles can now start. She went on the web, found a great job back home, found a great home, and had great Christmas with her family.

If we want to be successful in our relationships, we must first establish healthy views for ourselves. Just as we begin to be kind to ourselves and start to build compassion, we begin to stretch our hearts to those around us. We cannot know what love, understanding, and empathy are unless we do not place ourselves in the shoes of the other. It would help to become forgiving and honest towards yourself, to receive it and give it. When you become one with yourself and have established the steps you need to take to become higher vibrational, you begin to comprehend the real significance a person holds in your life. Your vibration and energy will tell you right away if something wrong is happening.

Just As The Plants Need Sunlight And Water To Grow, You Need Healing

If you want to heal another, you must first heal yourself. The process of healing is simple but needs you to be brave. I am sure you can do it. First, all you need to do is accept that you are a human and forgive yourself for your past mistakes. You need to understand that you can also have negative habits that will surface from time to time. But the way to deal with such emotions is first to acknowledge them. I do not mean speaking or doing anything which will harm your energy. What I mean is that you face them. Acknowledge that the problems exist, but there is a solution to every situation, and you will come out of it all.

When the emotions begin to surface, you let them ride through your body. I will tell you how you can channel them positively, which allows you to become stronger emotionally and spiritually. Pain or sorrow often takes place physically as well as emotionally. It is why it is always best to face it and deal with it as the feelings occur. If we do not care for ourselves and deal with the negative emotions, we will start carrying a heavier burden, and our vibration will be significantly affected. It can be damaging to our auras, and our energy becomes heavy not just for ourselves but also for those around us. Just as the plants need sunlight and water to grow, you need healing.

I will now help you understand ways you can deal with your negative emotions. When we witness or feel a negative emotion in our bodies, we tend to get angry or disappointed or reactive in a negative way. I would never tell you to distract yourself. As I had mentioned before, you need to channel it the right way. You need first to allow yourself to feel all of those emotions while beginning to do something you love most. Whenever such feelings start to surface, you take yourself to deal with yourself. If you enjoy cooking or baking, dancing, or painting; whatever it is that makes you feel relaxed and happy, start doing it. It is also therapeutic to write about what you are feeling.

If There Is Dark, There Is Light

When you do right by yourself and what you feel, it eventually stops sounding unpleasant, and then there is simply nothing to worry about. Pure emotion is always honest. While reflecting on the emotions, go back in time and try to find where the first time this feeling came to you, like in the story of my friend. Find the beginning, and then let it go. Meditate to let this pain or hurt be released to the universe and forgive all parties involved, including yourself. But do remember always to give yourself a sound conclusion. Tell yourself that if there is dark, there is light. And if there is black, there will be white. One cannot be without the other.

Keep in mind the answer to getting back to feeling happy, loving, grateful, and peaceful is by doing activities to raise your vibration. Any activity that makes you happy is awesome. Of course, all exercise activities are going to raise your emotions to happiness. Also, an activity that brings you pleasure like meditating by water, climbing a mountain rather than just sitting to absorb the view, painting, singing, making love with passion, best is hugging your loved one.

I have mentioned in earlier chapters that when we exercise or create movement, our physiology changes. As that happens, our brain produces the happy chemicals required for us to feel better. You feel better emotionally and physically; the pain which was about to take form in your body gets flushed out through the activity you perform.

Pick any activity you love or enjoy and make it a part of your routine. When you begin to cherish your own time and existence and feed it right, you learn to love and better understand yourself. You can solve your emotional and spiritual problems better, and as you do this; your overall vibration and productivity get better. Take all these steps as an act of healing. Remind yourself that you are letting your emotions surface to allow them to heal. Do not suppress them, but instead, get up and do what you enjoy. Focus on being alive and tuned into the moment. Let yourself flow and allow your body to release the negative sensations. Once you begin to feel lighter, you can gradually shift the negative to the positive. Practice gratitude at the end. Thank yourself for being able to be so brave and to be able to channel your emotions the right way. Above that, when you learn to deal with your feelings positively, you save yourself and your energy from getting affected and getting hurt or hurting someone.

There Is Yin To Every Yang, It Is Wrong With Every Right, And With The Heavy, There Comes Light

Let's take a breather and recall all that we have just learned about channeling the human emotions, transforming them into a cheerful expression, the human psyche, and the ego. We all are human, and we are bound to have defects in our personality, one way or another. But when we learn to acknowledge these defects and work toward healing ourselves, we understand the deeper roots of what causes them. This way, we begin to understand ourselves better and what works for us and what does not. When this happens, we become more enlightened and responsible for our actions. We keep our energy cleansed and light to complement our aura, ensuring that it does not weigh heavy for those around us. Also, remember all emotions are to guild us through life, not control us.

I know you are brave and have come too far to get caught up in this negative cycle. You have learned that there is yin to every yang, it is wrong with every right, and with the heavy, there comes light. You can manifest deeper levels of optimism in yourself. Once you are practicing it all, you become more and more joyous and free. You take accountability for the ego and what it can do to your relationships. You become wiser, you not only allow yourself to be forgiven, but you also express forgiveness and gratitude in your relationships. Judgment stops. If we talk about the need to become positively expressive in our relationships, especially with our partners, you will begin to see it as a tool that will help you make the best of the act of human expression.

Our bodies require us to feel loved and to give it to another. The energy we carry has a significant impact on our partners' life. This goes both ways. When you have a higher vibration and know the real value of healing, you become healthier and more patient towards your partner's healing process as well. We understand each person has the right to have their own life, personality, and path. We are not here to live it for them. We are here to share our life and guild but not control. In hard times, you will not become distant, but you will come closer to your partner. This will have a beneficial impact on your sex life too. You will enjoy it more and be able to feel compassion and affection in its purest form. We take sex for granted so quickly. If you truly understand that it can also be a form of more profound healing and the act of pure communication, you will begin to speak and hear the secrets of your soul and your partner's. Take your time and allow your partner to take their time as well. Cherish the moments you create during sex and let them heal you. To receive love, you must first give it.

Now, as you have learned how to channel your emotions and deal with ego, I have a task for you. I want you to evaluate yourself and see where you stand. The next time you encounter an argument or debate or can feel negative emotions surface, allow yourself to ask what is causing it. Before you react, understand whether the negativity is coming from you or the other and what you can do to make this situation better. Can you change your tone? Can you develop better words? Can you offer emotional or physical support to solve the problem? Analyze where you stand. Understand what you often tend to do wrong so you can begin to start working on all of these to heal better. Initially, it may start as a challenging process, but once you initiate to have better command over yourself and the situation, you will be very thankful. I assure you; it just not only saves your time and energy but keeps you away from saying or doing things which you may regret later.

Just as you will evaluate how you react to such a situation; I want you to see how you respond with yourself. How do you express negative emotions as they start to surface? Do you already do what you love and channel it positively? Or do you react and let your time go to waste? Even if you have been doing so in the past, it is okay. I'm here now, and with the complete guidance provided in this book, you will learn to deal with all of these situations. So, tell me, how you express? What is it that you would want to do to feel better? Why don't you do it? Trust me, everything is possible. You just must take a deep breather, think, and understand what you can do to serve yourself well. After all, to have a healthier life and relationships, you must first be sure that the relationship you have with yourself is vigorous.

CHAPTER 8

GOD: OUR HIGHER BEING

We humans have been feeding upon the delusion of independence ever since technological and cultural advancements have rapidly increased. We have become so caught up with running around chasing the material world when everything that needs to manifest dwells. We now perceive that we are not answerable to anyone and control everything that has to happen. We feel like we are the final decision-makers, not bound to our fates, and no higher power that we must turn to. It is ridiculous to believe all these things. Look around you. The skies, the mountains, the ocean, you; you in your beautiful and remarkable existence. From your fingertips to your toes, look at your magnetic structure. Was this your creation? We have begun to laugh at so many of the extraordinary aspects created by God. Instead of paying gratitude for it, we live in constant denial because it has been easier to abide within our comfort zones than to be among the brave ones who are honest. Are you the one to decide upon the breaths to take? Are you the one controlling time? Changing weathers, turning dawn to day and day to dusk? Do you have all the answers that you have been looking for? The obvious answer is no. Everything within us and around us is God.

Connection with Your Higher Being God & Spirituality

Our higher power is our ultimate spiritual Connection to God or the universe. The idea is not to let our emotions and ego control us and take away our ability to see miracles and live an extraordinary life. Learning to let go is the primary goal. It is so simple and challenging to let go of your fears and know God has your beautiful life all aligned. All you have to do is find your path and let the universe guild you with incredible miracles. You begin by taking baby steps.

As you have been practicing the pillars of energy and higher vibration, start talking to God. Look for him in the places where you have been searching for answers. Whenever you feel stuck or lost, speak to God, you will witness how easily things align for you. Following your religion and belief system can bring wisdom and experience for you as an intellect. Religion has been underestimated in so many ways due to the dogmatic conceptions imposed upon men and women. We always forget the spiritual advantages practicing religion can bring. You tend to find discipline within your routine if you start to pray daily. You were going to church, praying, bible study, retreats. They give you a more profound sense of belonging and strengthens your connection with God. Give your total ego over to God and trust his ways. You will see how beautifully everything unfolds for you. Feel God's love. Live for the moment, not for tomorrow, not even for the past – just today. Take it day by day, and you start to see how incredibly your life turns out.

The more modernized we are becoming, the more we lose sight of the most crucial life lessons. We came to this world to make a change. Be significant in our ways. Nothing is too much or too little. We need to find our balance. Stop controlling your world. Let miracles happen; they will, all the time if you let them. Look for clues, signs from your higher power - follow them. Once you open yourself up to receiving what the universe can offer to you, you will begin to comprehend everything differently. When you function at a higher vibration, you tend to have a gut feeling of everything being exactly right. In signs, people say, you can feel a lost one trying to tell you something (they probably are). That is another level of consciousness and higher vibration you can accomplish once you open yourself to the unique possibilities of this universe. Just don't worry. Live in the moment; trust that the signs will guide you. A lot of times, letting go is better for our mental health than holding on.

Connect to Your Higher Being: Let Go - Let God.

Now I will have to say this, letting go genuinely was the most challenging part of my spiritual growth. It was when I was tired of forcing the world to be my way. Grand jobs, controlling powerful men I loved, wanting life my way. I found out that many of my passions were rooted in my ego and past conditioning. Pain and fear also guide me to live in survivor mode. The time came when I needed to trust God. God had a better plan, and everything would be okay. I had to remind myself that I would not fall into an endless abyss and decided to take that step and trust a plan for myself and to live a peaceful life. My efforts were to let go and follow the clues. But first, you need to have a plan, a deep desire which you want to achieve. Make it vivid in your mind. Now dream about it. Write about it. Start working on the steps that pave a direction, not just a dream. It would be best if you had a happier life with no lousy energy robbers and mean people who choose to hurt you than lift you. That is everything in your life.

Surrounding yourself with the right minds and people who carry positive energy is especially important. If your job offers a pessimistic environment, change it. Many toxic aspects need to be flushed out of your routine once you start to manifest higher vibrations. You have to ensure that your spouse needs to be on board with the new you. All your relationships, family, or friends need to that you want to be happy, and all the negativities must be removed from your life. They will learn to be more respectful quickly as they will want to be around you. Setting your boundaries is not a bad thing. It also teaches you self-discipline. You want to avoid low vibrations - for example, this is what we want to stop and remove from our life. You want to make sure that you do not have a scattered brain. You want to be able to master what you truly desire.

Keep a lookout for overactive, over-reactive, negative thoughts that keep you worrying. You need to know what you can do and what not. If you do not start to be careful about what you feed your energy with, no one else will. Begin to focus on what works for your life when you begin to radiate. You will set an example among all of those around you. Now take the first step to move toward the path you were designed to follow.

God Dwells Within You

When you start to focus on your healing with the holistic approach, a lot that did not make sense before starts to fall in place. You learn to accept yourself in ways you could never have, and then you become more forgiving. You practice empathy more often, and people start to see themselves in you. You begin to give them a sense of comfort, which you had been longing to find in another. When you start to focus inwards, you see God. It is as simple as that. The more honest you are with yourself, the closer you are to God and those around you. It is genuinely a special feeling when you are done with the world's weight, and you start to focus on the moment entirely. Everything starts to align impeccably. You just have to open up and accept yourself as God's beautiful creations.

A big part of my spiritual path is my meditation. My meditation is hiking in the mountains, walking through the woods, wading in the ocean, or even just sitting on my back porch. You do not have to make it a formal activity, but rather it a close part of you. I tend to walk and let my head rattle with whatever it needs to process. I do not force or hang onto the emotions. I let them flow. And keep them moving out of me. I ask the universe or God to give me peace and help guide me with uncomfortable emotions. When I finally have a quieter mind, I can meditate. I always find a great meditation spot. I sit for however long I need to talk to a dead loved one, my guardian angel, and God. I always have a confident plan for what I want to achieve. It is not complicated. It is simple and straightforward.

As I have mentioned in the chapter on Exercise, you can also refer to it to become closer to your higher self. Many religions offer praying or mediating while incorporating exercises. These not only help you calm down, but they also flush out the negative energy and replace it with the positive. It becomes a sacred act of expression between you, yourself, and the angels. If you follow a belief system that infuses exercises as you pray, keep it a regular habit. Your vibration is likely to become higher than what your body has been familiar with.

There are several other ways to calm your mind down and achieve the highest levels of consciousness. For some, it is deep underwater scuba diving where you have yourself liberated within the blue. You focus on your breathing and on keeping your body light. It enables you to let go of the toxicity developed over time, and you become as light as a feather when you come out. Similarly, you can also focus on aromatherapy. Get your favorite candles scented or even without. Every morning meditate slowly on the aroma you like and inhale and exhale as gently as you can. You begin to create a calm ambiance around you, which helps you settle.

The Art of Law of Attraction

I mentioned in the earlier chapters how incredible the art of the law of attraction is. It does indeed do wonders. I call it art because you must believe in it to make it work. You must understand to focus on what you truly desire and place positive attention on it. Positive attention means that you start being grateful for all that you have incurred, and whatever comes your way to open doors to what you truly desire, pay thanks to the Lord and your angels. Yes, the angels. Every individual is born with a guiding angel. You can take help from these angels, and they will guide you and clear the path for you. Manifest your path and dreams by raising your vibrations and praying regularly.

One of the most useful ways is to make a list of the top ten dreams and then leave it up to the attraction law. Build your friend circle with the right people with the right energy. Pray, every moment that you can. Be grateful for the moment, talk to your guardian angels, and ask for guidance.

It may seem like it is a lot of work, and perhaps it will be too, but the reward is priceless. If you do not do the work, higher vibrations may not serve you as they should. All miracles come, but you need to do the job. I had terrible credit and no money to buy one. I trusted that my higher power or angles would guide me to a more peaceful life. I got in my car started driving around, and a home that I had been calling and calling the realtor came into focus. A lady was cleaning the front door windows. I got out of the car and introduced myself. I let her know I have been calling for weeks to view this rental. The lady told me she was the owner and apologized on the realtor's behalf for being unresponsive. We talked, and we got along so well we signed a rental agreement right then.

We moved into the home a week later. The money came to me to handle the security deposit and rent. I needed a job, so I walked down Main Street and talked to many store owners for a job. Then a perfect French pastry restaurant required help. A sweet, fun job just opened for me. It is important to realize not to get all wound up and just let the world and angles around you help. They will if you let them. The key here is to give gratitude to the universe or God for all the fantastic gifts he is giving you.

Make a list of what you want in your life and what is unnecessary in your life. I make a top ten list all the time, which changes as I achieve my goals. It includes my long-term dreams, my financial dreams, and my current needs. The key is to constantly review that list because it creates a recall within my mind and pushes me ahead to work toward them. I have a journal to go back to and check how I have grown and achieved over the years.

Connection to God or higher Connection

The most important is hearing when God talks to us. I don't live in the past. Forget the pain, learn to let it go, Fight now, right here. Do not look for the future. Do not dwell on the anticipation of betterment. Do not ask questions like 'when will I be happier?' Stop that now. Right now, stop this very moment. Ask yourself, "Is everything ok?" Look around you and feel the moment. Is everything okay? 99% of the time, that moment is simply fine. Take a deep breath, feel the moment, and smile. Thank God for those moments. Thank God for today, name all the great good things that are happening. Kids, work, friends, health, home, just say thanks for all the daily moments throughout the day. Say thanks all day long to God. Just stop and say thank you for today. It will give you warmth and a sense of peace. Trust me.

It will bring you into the present, not the past that we can't change or the future, which is just a dream. It also is a way to ground you to the earth frequencies and the current moments. It is helpful throughout your day. You can get yourself high or off-balance, and this will bring you back to the current moment. To follow your right path, happiness, health, and giving, you need to be present to receive the gifts, clues, strength, and joy that are always there for you. You must be present. You will find it beneficial because the negative ego of others trying to rob you of your energy and make you feel bad will no longer impact you. It will make you healthy, and other bad stuff can't affect you – it will just roll off you. It is so cool how it works and how easy it is to stay healthy. Try it.

When you walk into hostile environments with people like parents, bosses, ex-spouses, etc., your energy might drain. Ground yourself to the moment, take deep breaths, Thank God, and smile. Then watch how this changes the expected outcome. Stay in the moment yourself. When we are not emotionally responsive, we are stronger, happier, and more comfortable, feeling like we've transformed into another person. Positive energy is always stronger than negative energy. Energy stealing can't happen. Your war with energy stealing and ego triggers stop.

When clues come around you, watch for them. They can be in any form. They can be on TV; several of the same things keep popping up in different ways. Have an urge to be spontaneous after you have been thinking about a change. Follow the signs, a new home, a new job, take a walk. You will be amazed by how the miracles will happen right when you need them. I have many times needed a home or a job or money to pay a bill. It always happens and finds its way to me. I may not know the real outcome, but I know it is right and on the right path. I just have a comfortable, calming feeling. Not a nervous, uncomfortable feeling.

It is always necessary for you to evaluate your current self with the changes you want to manifest. Ask yourself a couple of questions that define your current lifestyle regarding your friends, family, and job. Start to plan out how you want to change it and what you want as the final goal. Craft a path for yourself with baby steps that you can take and sometimes be spontaneous. The universe can be very adventurous, too, when it comes to your calling. You might know what is written for you next. Trust me. It will be spectacular. Just keep evaluating yourself and pay gratitude for all the steps and stages you have achieved. It was on my list to reach out to you. Because, like you, I also want to change and allow you to bring the best out of yourself. It is a beautiful cycle that we can create—life is full of energy and purpose. Trust yourself and trust God. Your hard work has already started to pay off remarkable. Just you watch.

CHAPTER 9

LET'S PULL THIS ALL TOGETHER

Consistency is Key

My journey had many highs and lows, but I established a way to have the option to comprehend the remarkable degrees of energy. I learned how to develop my thoughts into higher vibrations. During my more youthful years, I was informed that I was expected to carry on with life's good and bad times to get an appropriate hold on vibrational energy. I have effectively figured out how to live through some difficult stretches, and fortunately, each time, I developed further. My troublesome encounters caused me to comprehend what self-enlightenment is and how every last one of us is equipped for mending our internal identity. It's a remarkable process of how you can transform your torment and show yourself the best approach to escape the haziness in life.

physical health	emotional happiness	mental focus	spiritual purpose
The foundation of all other dimensions of energy, physical energy is comprised of sleep, fitness, nutrition, and intermittent daytime rest and renewal.	Emotional energy is about learning to cultivate the specific emotions associated with high performance, because how people feel profoundly influences how they perform.	Mental energy is about learning to focus in an absorbed way and switching intentionally between tactical and big-picture thinking.	Spiritual energy is the energy derived from serving something larger than oneself.

We are moving to a higher vibrational frequency in our everyday world currently. It is common for our youth to see and experience different dimensional perspectives. They are all raising the bar and are way more open to higher energy fields. This, in turn, opens them up to healthier and happier existences. I am sharing with you the secret to how you can get past life's pains and live a happier, healthier life by raising your vibrational energy. Live your chosen path.

The key is consistency. Take everything I have shown you about the four pillars and set a plan that works for you. Change your diet to be alkaline, exercise in ways that make you smile, learn to use emotions to guide you, not control you, let go at times of emotional pain and fear, and connect to your higher power. It is essential always to be clear of your dreams, your path, and your life.

Holistic Healing Over Western Medicine

While we all may live in the same world, our experiences and outlook on life depend on our energetic vibration. People who have higher vibrational energy enjoy a far more empowered and optimistic view of life. They tend to work on a deep love-based emotional level— those who vibrate on a lower-level experience more negative emotion. Our body's vibrational energy flow affects our health and mental state. Your mind, body, and soul are all affected by four pillars: diet, exercise, emotions, ego, and your higher power. The medical world is all about dealing with the problem and just giving you chemicals to handle, and mask, or poison to heal.

What is breaking down in your body to create the medical issue? Dealing with the medical issue with the current conventional medicinal approach is like putting a bandage on a gash. We need to get to the underlying problem to get the body back healing itself. Like I said, your health and happiness are all tied to your diet, exercise, ego or emotions, and your higher power. My goal is to help you understand quite literally how we can take control of our own life and body. To demonstrate how natural energy vibrations work on the mind, body, and soul. If you give a flower a lot of water, nutrition, and sunlight, it will grow strong and healthy. I told you before a plant with no water, no care, and no sun will not live. We are very much the same, but extremely complicated. The most important is how close you are to your higher source or God.

All these pillar areas Diet, Exercise, Ego/mind, and God are all very much needed to be understood if you want to learn how they raise or lower the vibrational energy within your body. I believe that the ego is lower vibration energy and causes harm to the body. Lack of physical strength and oxygen affects our ability to move awful stuff out of our bodies. It makes the body hold onto toxicity and poison, which, in time, starts damaging us. These emotions come from conditioning in your past. We want to be at an energy level that your body naturally cures itself. Is your body now at a vibrational level that facilitates healing? It is a stage where your body can naturally heal and rebuild itself. Staying bodily fit and eating clean and healthy are the primary keys to keeping the body vibrating in a full heal mode.

A Trip to the Four Pillars

We have established that diet, exercise, emotions, and your higher power is the four pillars. They can all have higher and lower levels of energy vibrations. Each of these is important for raising your whole body and soul's vibrational energy to a point conducive to a healthy and happy life. The main aim for us is to understand how to integrate higher power on each pillar. I would ask you to question yourself to gain more insight. What is energy? How does it impact our lives? We know everything is energy in one way or another. As discussed in earlier chapters, it is the central source of our being. We can now achieve serendipity through life. When we dig deeper to understand the power of energy, we give ourselves the chance to be tuned in and have synchronicity with the universe. Of course, *life* is the key. We dig deeper and understand the reliable sources are pillars of energy we have achieved so far: diet, exercise, emotions, and our higher power. We have the ability within ourselves to create the miracles we could only imagine.

The higher power is a higher vibration. To improve the four pillars, we must understand the link between them and compliment them in a more fulfilling life. The first pillar is the diet.

We know that diet is not just the careful intake of food items we consume. It revolves around all that we are to consume daily. It is also the content we go through on social media or the books we read to feed our intellectual appetite. We apply the forms of meditation in our routines, be it religious or not, and finally, the type of food we take and the amount we consume it in. It is essential to be selective with such food items. It is also necessary to understand that a good alkaline diet is the key to a healthier body. Diet revolving around intellectual and nutritional intakes, spirituality plays the most crucial role. If you have attained a spiritual balance in life, you will most likely gain an emotional balance. The importance may vary according to life experiences. To be fully inclined toward the mind, body, and soul in a manner that your vibration is in the right direction, you may be on the path to embracing spirituality. You can perceive beyond logic. Hence, your steps to a spiritual path have taken place before you have acknowledged the same.

After achieving a healing body, you will enjoy life waiting for you; peaceful, loving, and healthy. This understanding of the four pillars of vibrational energy will help you take full control of your life via a simple explanation of how your bodies vibrate at various levels to cater to different experiences. It is essential to understand your diet's bearing, what shape you are in, how you handle stresses and emotional pain to have your body's energy rise. Let us look into the diet plan we had discussed earlier and see where we stand. I was hoping you could make notes on your daily routine and your media and food consumption intake. Be honest and create a chart of all you have been consuming. Now make a chart for your ideal diet with the prescribed diet plans you wish to follow. Evaluate the difference and make honest notes on what it is that you need to do. What acidic and alkaline foods do you need to remove? When you begin to be honest with the alterations, you will discover many areas that need to be worked on.

As I recall mentioning earlier, my initial healing began with my diet when I had gotten cancer. To ensure that I was consuming the right foods and water intakes to get my system running right, I began to use the power of consistency. It did not just flush out all the toxins I needed to stay active, but the diet also played a crucial role in aging less and staying focused.

The Harmony Exercise Can Bring

Exercise is the repetitive movement of your body. Be it through a gym routine, yoga, dance, or a sport. If you stay in motion that creates harmony for your physical well-being, you will be spiritually and physically vibrational. With diet and exercise acting as the key pillars that add value to our physical well-being, emotional stability soon follows. However, a dynamic equilibrium does not refer to being low or suppressing emotions. It is the act of being vulnerable in the right manner. You channel your negative emotions intelligently. You learn to acknowledge lower energy levels that are hurting you and do not let them affect your wellbeing. Think of your body as a processor or a machine that takes the raw emotion you feel and turns it into a sensation that allows you to create better situations for yourself. We have understood how to transform our negative energy into health through exercise.

All the elements of nature can complement our fitness routines in a significant manner if we give it the kind of attention it requires to amplify our vibration. Trust me, without exercise, we cannot live to our fullest. We really cannot enjoy the fruits that God has given to us in the form of our physical self. It requires training and an open mind that practices gratitude to be able to achieve that. Once you make it a habit to do so, you will experience the miracles you have been waiting to have. Keep walking through with me. You are doing an excellent job. Just some more steps left, and you can achieve all. I assure you.

Before we step out of the wonderments exercise and nature can bring for us, I have a task for you. I want you to be able to become healthier and fit as you raise your vibration to the fullest. For this, you need to read your routine as a mentor. Be critical but know that we have the solutions to solve all the worries. The cure lies within you, always has and always will. Check yourself and see where you stand. Analyze your routine and understand how much you exercise or if you exercise at all. What creative ways can you bring in more movement to your life and create a more beautiful sync with yourself? There may be many as we learned how we could add exercise so quickly to our daily routines. Please keep it simple enough to do regularly.

I know you have the strength to keep up with the four pillars – you are to make miracles happen and enjoy a satisfying life. Love yourself and your body. Give it all the gifts it deserves. Observe life with more gratitude, and you witness how everything you had been waiting for will come to you like a magnet. I would advise you to start exercising the soonest you can if you have not started already. A task for you: What is the daily creatives moves or exercise which you have now added to your routines? I was hoping you could come up with five activities that you commit to yourself to do regularly. Be sure to incorporate deep breathing, which enhances your overall experience. Once you have come up with the exercises you can do, why not give them each a name? That way, you will remember them, and if they are useful, you can also teach them to your friends or family.

The Impact of Emotion & Ego

Understanding how to move through your emotions to guide you and not to control you is also crucial. Fear, selfishness, guilt, apathy, grief, anger, and pride are going to be a part of your life. Learning how to heal and move past your fears and past pains is what you need to do. We do not want to let our emotions control our world. They just guide us to make the best decision to follow our path. Let us understand sentiments enough to ensure that we are not a victim anymore. You can be at an emotional level so low that it is close to death. I have been taught that 0 to 200 is where all negative dynamic behavior vibrates all levels lower than 200 are harming us somehow, and that is where illness is generated. We need to understand our emotions and learn to raise ourselves above 200, i.e., courage. I repeat, it is then that we can self-heal.

Here is a reflective task for you; tell me where you currently stand. Take the sum of your negative levels and positive levels and keep them separate. Which side is winning? Where do you feel that you need to work more? If your positive emotions are higher, it means you are in a good spot. You have been healing and have also become spiritually rational. If not, how do you think you can improve? Come up with small sticky notes for each day and make small goals to practice holistic healing further, so you know that you have reached a higher vibration. The important part to always remember is that healing your pains, fear, and emotions are all in the past. They all have a starting point to which they began. A big part of meditation is taking an emotion and going back in time to each time it has ruled its ugly head and letting it go. Forgive yourself and the person involved. There will be a beginning to where this emotion started. When you find the beginning, let it go and forgive yourself. There will be a major relief at that time. Give it to the universe and breath. You will feel an amazing sense of peace after.

You will now start to feel higher vibrations that enable you to have a more welcoming aura. The aura you develop will add more meaning to your personality and manifest a lot more for you that paves a successful life direction. The more you have command over the four pillars, the higher vibration you will have. The more enlightenment you will achieve through holistic healing. After all, the primary purpose of writing this was for you to heal through my recovery and help heal the world one person at a time.

The Daily Practice for Higher Vibration

(Higher Vibrations)

You may be wondering what these notions stand for. Ego & Emotion, Color Cleansing Basket and Sweat? It is simple; they are the four pillars combined into the perfect strategy to adapt accordingly. We all want to ensure that we are consistent with the four pillars, so I came up with a few ways to be done. Let's begin!

Ego & Emotion: There is no cure and answer to emotional healing and intelligence like a morning meditation. Once you begin your day right, the chances are you will have more command over the rest of your day. You begin your day with a morning prayer or meditation session where you let your body move forward and step into the shoes of an evolved version of you—a calmer and saner one who is collective and affirmative.

Diet: We all know it clearly; *we are what we eat.* The diet section entails the kind of foods you will be consuming. Other than that, the reason why we call it "The Green Cleansing Basket" is because it is to flush out the undesired while raising your vibrations the right way. Green is a color that symbolizes holistic healing and spirituality; hence with better visualization, we can live fresher. Be creative with your life, guys. You only get it once. Live it the right way and cherish yourselves as you have always wished to. The time has come that you make it right with who you are meant to be.

Exercise: I am sure by now you know how to balance your chakras and what to do if they feel blocked. Making Yoga a habit while infusing the exercises you can stick to for a stronger spiritual appetite, you know how to infuse the right movement. Other than that, we have discussed before the many ways to incorporate exercises into your daily routine. Once you have been actively doing the exercises, you will know the changes are remarkable. Like the meal plan template, I have added at the end of the chapter, you can also plan for your exercises. Keep these plans in your sight as constant reminders. You are only human, and we all can forget a thing or two. Yet, to avoid that from happening, make it a habit of sticking your plans up. You may also inspire your family members to do the same. Once you take the lead with what needs to be done, you will set an incredible example.

Higher Vibrations = Your Purpose: When you have achieved the routine where you can invest what it takes to keep higher vibrations, you will know how to channel all the areas in life more effectively. However, this does not mean you will not have any bad days. The bad days are there to teach us. Just do not take them as an escape to become who you do no longer serve to be. Let them be a reminder of good days and light at the end of the tunnel. Like the law of attraction and manifesting philosophies, we speak of the need to be sourced through energies. Now you already know how that is done. It is now time we understand how crucial it is for us to self-heal. Why do we need to do that? Because we want to sustain all the best that we have learned and created.

Self-Heal to Self-Sustain

Your greater power is your spirituality. It is the link we all need to this earth and universe and all souls. When we can feel like a part of all life, we grow a sense of cohesion. You must recognize the impact you have on the people and world around you, and your being is invisible yet inescapable. Remember what you think, say, and project outwardly into the world will make it healthy or unhealthy. Deeds such as meditation, praying, long meditational hikes, and so many others can help ground oneself and achieve balance and learn to let go. This process will give you the calmness to ask the universe or God to guild you and help bring on the miracles you need.

Now that you have some insight and clarity on energy flow, I would like you to take some time from your busy schedules, ponder over something crucial. I would like you to review your energy, look at your issues carefully, and reflect on how negative energy or low energy affects your life. Once you figure out all the above, get to work. Make some necessary changes in your growth and rise kindly. I believed in myself, and now I am residing in you to excel, be the supreme being you were created to be, and live your life to the fullest.

I want you to keep track of your behavior and analyze if your exhibited action is the reaction to any raw thoughts. See why you feel a certain way that you do. Understand what helps you in clearing your chakras and helps your energy circulate better. Take notes of what exercises or food intake help you overcome a situation and rejuvenate your inner life. One must practice self-awareness to manifest holistic healing and higher vibration. Evaluate where you have performed in the last thirty days and set goals for the next month. The road to enlightenment begins when you start to study yourself before anything else. When you start to see what raises you or lowers you, you have the keys to healing yourself even more positively. Keep going as you are, and I can tell you that by the time you finish this book, you will experience a remarkable change that will illuminate your entire world. That is, of course, if you open yourself up to the change.

I have worked on a template that you can adapt to. You can construct yours on a weekly diet chart. I know it is not easy to stick to one thing, but you will have the space to be creative and realistic with what you want to consume regularly. Step by step, you can work on reducing or increasing a particular item. After that, once you have your plans in front of you, evaluate them monthly. This way, you will be able to stay on track with whatever you have planned consistently. I have told you before; your life is your canvas. Paint it as it would please you. You have all the necessary elements given, like the paints and the brushes. It's your chance to make the painting you always wanted. Just do not forget to be gentle and forgiving with yourself.

CHAPTER 10

EXTRA WAYS TO RAISE YOUR ENERGY FIELDS PART 1: THE FRUITS FOR HEALING

Choose Your Healing

We always come across books, movies, reviews, or even advertisements based on the different healing forms—all prescribing how it will work and what you should do with it. But no one tells us how to understand what you need and what will suit you. We all are built differently, and everyone needs his or her time to experience and understand what will help most. There is nothing wrong with selling a particular aspect to make a living, but what about the greater good, and how do you understand it if you need it or not? It is always best to begin your healing by being patient with yourself and knowing that it will take time. Try whatever you need to step by step and see what fits you best. See what makes your vibrations rise instantly and what kind of healing and routine you can keep up with. By giving yourself time in the right direction, you will conquer what you may find impossible.

The Law of attraction

I have said it before, and I'll repeat it, Law of Attraction is real, and it does wonders. Once you begin to embark on the incredible journey towards true enlightenment in the Law of Attraction, you must understand that you can apply it to your life, and it can be active if it is performed the right way. The practices and beliefs in this law have been igniting the lives of great individuals throughout history. Hundreds of years ago, the Law of Attraction was first thought to have been taught to man by the immortal Buddha. It is believed he wanted it to be known that 'what you have become is what you have thought.' It is a belief that is deeply intrinsic in the Law of Attraction. This means you can indeed manifest your desires by the amount of attention you place on them.

As this concept became widely known to Western culture, *Karma* became a widespread belief throughout numerous societies. Like I tell you, *every action causes an opposite and equal reaction,* Karma, plays the same role in our lives. Over the centuries, it has been a common understanding that what you give out to the world is what can return to your own life in the end. What you reap is what you sow. The kind of energy and vibrations you will develop and establish around yourselves; is the kind of life you will attract. To receive good in life, one must be fair and do good. You cannot expect greatness to happen for you if you have not intended to spread greatness out to the world. It all goes both ways in life. You need to share the fruits to get more in return. The concept has been so common among many for an awfully long time. It demonstrates that the idea of the influence of attraction is not new. It is already familiar to many of us in multiple ways.

The Law of Attraction's main principles can also be discovered in the teachings of many civilizations and religious groups. As discussed before, The Law of Attraction and its values have been seen historically. Many women and men who have left their mark on this world have shown the Law of Attraction to be one of the most significant powers on earth. Numerous well-loved poets, artists, scientists, and great thinkers convey this message through their many works. There are so many celebrities that practice this Law and have complete faith in it – Oprah Winfrey, Jim Carrey, and Denzel Washington. There are plenty of success stories surrounding The Law of Attraction. In earlier chapters, you read how I could manifest great things by placing the proper attention and vibration. So, can you!

However, there is an upside to this concept. The most thought-provoking part of acknowledging and accepting the truth of what the Law of Attraction has to offer is realizing that every single one of your decisions in life, good and bad, has been shaped by you alone. For many, this can be a bitter pill to swallow, especially if you feel that you or your loved ones have been dealt some harsh blows in life. However, once you have indeed come to understand the valid key behind the Law of Attraction, you can be renewed with hope and courage in the overpowering knowledge that you are free to take charge of your life and free yourself forever from the cycle of fear, worry, and negativity, which has held you back for too long. When you begin to understand this and liberate yourself from all the negativity, you'll be as light as a feather!

The Secret Fruits & Seeds

I know that we keep discussing diet and food consumption on repeat, but believe me, *you are what you eat.* Fruits like apples, oranges, pears, papaya, and many others have a higher vibration than processed juices. One bowl of fresh fruits can not only keep you healthy, but it will serve as great nourishment to your mind. Fresh Organic fruits and vegetables also play a crucial role. Organic is just not a trend, but it serves as a great source of energy in reality. Organic vegetables and products contain exceedingly high vibration, which is tapped directly from the sun's strength. We often forget the Sun's power and how it can impact our immune system. God created us to take the best from natural aspects that exist for us.

Ancient history bears testimony to the fact that nature itself has the best of medicines that can be lifesaving as well as life changing. They are energizing, alkaline, and good for the system. Cooking any food can destroy its nutrients and natural enzymes. Therefore, anything consumed raw contains high vibration. But make sure you clean them properly before the intake. Raw Salt is another excellent source of high vibration. The original Himalayan salt, pink salt, or any form of unprocessed salt contains very high energy. Natural Celtic sea salt is also known for its high nutrient and energy value. Fresh fruits carry high vibration that detoxifies your body, increases your light quotient, and enhances your life frequency. One glass of fresh celery juice early in the morning can work wonders for your body.

I call this nature's gifted drink; drinking fresh coconut water for ten days will make you feel fresh. It will also help elevate your mood and increases the happiness proportion. Peanuts, hazelnuts, sweet almonds, and sunflower seeds contain extremely high frequency; they are rich in fiber and energy. As a routine, you can make them your evening snack. The last but most important source of vibration is clean water. Our body is composed of 60% water, and our earth is also formed of the same. Thus, if you always stay well hydrated, you will never feel lethargic and have bright, glowing skin. Try it and see for yourself. 10-12 glasses of water daily will be enough for improving your internal and external health. A little bit of awareness can make your everyday food a miracle. Express a little appreciation to the universe before eating, and never forget to appreciate the one who cooked the meal for you. Your kind thoughts can energize the food and raise the vibration of those who eat it.

The Chiropractic Care

I am sure you never assumed that chiropractic care could boost energy levels. Isn't that reserved for injuries and other problems, as one may think? What many do not know is that chiropractic care can do wonders for your energy levels in a completely natural way. Why? The underlining problem can be your spine, which in turn affects your nervous system. One of the most common causes of low energy levels and fatigue is an unstable spine. When the spine is misaligned, it can impair the balance in your entire body. A crooked spine affects your posture, thus allocating weight unequally and forcing your body to work more to keep everything in order. It may seem insignificant, but when this problem continues and is left unsolved, even the smallest imbalance adds up to hours of wasted energy. You know, our nervous system is equally essential for your energy levels. Energy flows through nerves, which distribute it throughout your body. When your spine is aligned adequately, your energy levels will be balanced. But, when the spine isn't aligned correctly, it causes impaired energy flow, thus contributing to tiredness.

The Acupuncture

Private acupuncture sessions can allow for a more profound healing experience. Practitioners can also treat the body areas such as the back and abdomen, which cannot be accessed right away. Depending on the condition, practitioners may also use other electrical stimulation techniques, cupping, gua sha, moxibustion, and tuning forks. People may find this an odd form of healing, but Acupuncture helps in so many ways. It not only stimulates your blood flow but allows your nerves to perform better too. One cannot comprehend the wonderments of a particular aspect until and unless we have fully indulged ourselves in it. You cannot have the full experience unless you are willing to try ultimately.

Reiki

I have discussed this a bit before, and you may already have been aware. A Reiki practitioner goes through and clears your energy meridians "chakras" that may be blocked. When energy blockages are present, we experience a change in our hormones and other health areas that may cause long-term illnesses. Meaning the body is not at ease or running efficiently. We need to rid our bodies of all the ailments that can exist in our system. It may be bizarre to assume that the very cure dwells within us, but it is a fact. However, we feed our bodies and treat them, the result reflects instantly. Sometimes it can be right away, and sometimes it takes time. You can control your consumption, and you can add value to your healing and higher vibrations by practicing Reiki.

The Miraculous Crystal Healing

You may have seen in many movies or read in novels that crystals play a role in the energy surrounding us. You may have noticed how crystals and stones are used to cure ailments in many cultures. Well, it's not taboo, nor is it unreal. It works. Crystal healing harnesses and focuses the power of Mother Nature. These gemstones look pretty to the naked eye, but on higher planes, they are balancing and assisting our energy bodies. As if some higher power and force wants to help keep us in alignment. If you investigate this, you will realize that there are many different kinds of stones. Every category has its own effects, and it is so interesting to study. Why not give it a shot to see if it may be your kind of healing?

Inferred sauna

I happen to enjoy this one personally. I love how my body's radiation is treated differently. It allows me to flush out all the toxins and embrace this soothing feeling which follows. It is different from the traditional sauna. Infrared saunas do not heat the air around you. Instead, they use infrared lamps (that use electromagnetic radiation) to warm your body directly. Drink water. Make sure you are hydrated before going into an infrared sauna. Drink a glass of water before your session. You can also bring water into the sauna, especially if you are sensitive to high heat. You choose the temperature. So, this is not something you would have to force yourself into or would need resistance for. It's easy to go along with. The average temperature for an infrared sauna ranges from 100°F to 150°F, with beginners starting at the lower end and more experienced users at the higher end. If this is your first time, begin with 100°F. You may want to stay at this temperature for a few sessions. You can always increase the temperature each session until you reach 150°F.

How do you determine the length of time? Well, for first-time users, start with 10 to 15 minutes. You can add time for each session until you reach the suggested time of 20 to 30 minutes. Saunas come with a timer, so make sure to set it. You do not want to stay in there too long and risk becoming dehydrated. How you dress is your choice. Some people will wear bathing suits, while others prefer to go in naked. You can always take your session to relax, read, meditate, listen to music, or visit with friends. Just do not go to sleep. After the session is over, it is suggested that you take your time and let your body cool down. Once cooled down, feel free to take a shower or bath. Just make sure you are drinking plenty of water. It can cause dehydration, but that is only if your system is lacking water. You know how crucial water is. You must have the appropriate intake.

Meditation

Every individual that I have come across has a different meaning to what meditation is. But what they all had in common was how crucial it is. What is it to meditate, and how do we do it? It is a sacred act that does not require us to be in any position or anything. It is useful if you have your space and area while meditating, but it is not necessary. You can still meditate without being alone or in a particular manner. Once you have complete command over your breath and concentration, you can do it anywhere, anytime. It enables you to become calmer and focus more. Meditation is simply a tool that you can apply to any sort of healing you are practicing. If you add meditation to anything you do, the experience becomes more fulfilling, but the results are more effective. This tool is something that should be a part of your routine for at least 15 minutes daily. When you begin to accomplish the benefits, you will understand how you can make it a part of so many things that come your way.

The Enchanting Solfeggio Music

Vibration also corresponds to emotions. When we identify with emotions such as anger, hatred, jealousy, guilt, paranoia, and self-loathing, we lower our vibration. On the other hand, when we stop identifying with these emotions and instead see them only as energy fluctuating within us, we begin to experience "high vibration" states such as love, peace, gratitude, creativity, and self-fulfillment. It's important here to remember that there's nothing wrong with feeling any type of emotion, including painful ones. Unfortunately, many new-age writers use the term "low vibration" to condemn and spiritually bypass emotions such as anger or grief. Ironically, charging these emotions generates more fear and resistance within the psyche, which further solidifies a "low vibrational" state.

Solfeggio Frequencies:

Listen to these 10 frequencies during meditation to amplify the experience -

174 Hertz - Removes Pain
285 Hertz - Influences Energy Field
396 Hertz - Liberates you of fear & guilt
417 Hertz - Facilitates Change
432 Hertz - Miracle Tone of Nature
528 Hertz - Repairs DNA
639 Hertz - Heals Relationships
741 Hertz - Awaken Intuition
852 Hertz - Attracts Soul Tribe
963 Hertz - Connect with Light & Spirit

While the best way to experience high vibration states such as love and bliss is to stop identifying and attaching to thoughts and emotions, there are helpful catalysts that help center your energy. One of these catalysts is known as the Solfeggio Frequencies. The Solfeggio Frequencies are a series of 6 electromagnetic musical tones that the Gregorian Monks used when they chanted in meditation. Re-experienced in 1974 by Dr. Joseph Puleo. The Solfeggio Frequencies are said to deeply penetrate the conscious and subconscious mind, encouraging inner healing. Dr. Puleo was intuitively led to rediscover these healing frequencies in the Book of Numbers (a book in the Hebrew Bible), using a numerological technique to decipher the six repeating codes he found. The result was the rediscovery of the Solfeggio Frequencies. Nikola Tesla once said: *If you only knew the magnificence of the 3, 6, and 9, then you would hold the key to the universe.* Fascinatingly, these three numbers form the root vibration of the six Solfeggio Frequencies.

Other Ways to Raise your Vibration

Books can have a very high vibrational impact. Pinterest has great advice on books with high energy. All the high VE and holistic books I have read always get me feeling excited with so much energy. I Love it. Then, I love reading a great novel to take me away is a great feeling. Music is an amazing way to raise your vibrational field quickly. Turn up the music. Music is the easiest way for me to feel happy and grateful, to calm and meditative. My normal quiet time is solfeggio frequency music. It depends on what I need to balance or heal. I chose the right frequency level and meditated on this wonderful music. The other cool way is to get happy and feel happy and great is to turn up the great tunes. I will be driving to work, and a great song comes on. I just sing my heart away. Try it the next time you feel mad or not your happiest. Get your groove on and dance to the rhythm.

EXTRA WAYS TO RAISE YOUR ENERGY FIELDS PART 2: WATER MEDITATION – SET YOUR INTENTIONS IN THE WATER

The Importance of Water Meditation

This is a fun and beautiful way of life. If you understood the secrets that water could bring to us, you would find the cure to so many ailments and issues through it. You see, water takes up all our energy. It can carry our vibration by having an effect that reflects our daily lives. At the end of this chapter, I will tell you how it works. For instance, you have chosen to raise two potted plants, one that you lovingly grow reciting poetry and the other that you sneer at and send all your worst thoughts. The plant that you nurture and care for and spoke lovingly to always seemed to thrive. As adults, as yogis, as practitioners of healthy eating and meditation, we understand the science behind positive affirmations and good vibrations.

H_2O has been placed next to high vibrational positive affirmations. It can create molecules with beautiful hexagonal shapes. This is the work of Japanese scientist Masaru Emoto, who believed that *water was the blueprint of our reality and that our vibrations and intentions could shape the water molecules*. Emoto concluded that the molecules of bad-intentioned water were jumbled and fractionated, while the water molecules that had received positive sense were beautiful and structured. Why should this matter to you? Because you are 60% water, my love. Positive intention changes you on a molecular level. Hence, vibration with water goes hand in hand. You need water the most. Water adds purity to your entire system. What is magical is that you can "create" this purity by placing the right intentions or, let us say, meditating to water. There is sacred geometry present in the molecular structure that water takes when influenced by the right intention. You know there are water visionaries? It is a remarkable thing to have come across. You can even test why they have so much faith in water healing. You can place it on your water bottle to raise your water's vibration and your life. After this chapter, my question will be, what were you doing before deciding to extend the planet's pulse?

The Beginning of Water Healing

Water healing does begin with our environment and how we would like to see it. Above that, I know we often do not have control over our surroundings and how they should appear to us, but the way to be with water meditation personally is not that hard either. Our Environment shapes our experience, so the more intention we devote to considering the senses, the better. You can include elements like a candle, a stone from the ocean, a botanical oil, fresh flowers, and a cold glass of sparkling water. I cannot emphasize enough the importance of this step! No one wants to roast like a lobster in the tub — it is not a good look. To attain the deepest levels of relaxation, I draw a hot bath, but not scalding. Like with the infrared sauna, you can manage the temperature for this too. Imagine slowing downtime as you enter the water — almost as if you are slipping into a liminal space where time ceases to exist. We begin to receive intuition and sensory experience as we slow down to the speed of nature and elemental wisdom. Your heart is the core of your existence, the drum that beats your unique rhythm and harmony. Sound travels differently within the water, so listen and hear the subtle sounds that typically allude to our attention. Connect with your pulse, breathe deeply into space at your center, and open to its wisdom. It will be a magical experience. Let it take you away.

Hydrotherapy

Hydrotherapy relies on its mechanical and thermal effects to induce healing. It takes benefit of the body's reaction to cold or hot stimuli, the pressure exerted by water, the protracted application of heat, and the sensation of the water. These sensations and effects are then carried more profoundly into the skin by nerves. When this happens, these sensations stimulate the immune system, thus influencing the release of stress hormones while improving digestion, circulation, and blood flow and reducing the body's sensitivity to pain. In most circumstances, heat is used to soothe and quiet the body while slowing down internal organs' activity.

On the other hand, cold is used to invigorate and stimulate, thus increasing the body's internal activity. Therefore, if you are suffering from anxiety and tense muscles, you should bathe with hot water. If you feel stressed out and tired, you should shower with hot water, followed by a short cold shower. This stimulates the mind and body. When you are underwater, for example, in a pool or a bath, you experience some kind of lightness. The water relieves the body of gravity's effects. Also, water induces a hydrostatic effect, as well as a massage-like feeling, as it kneads your body. Moving water stimulates the skin's touch receptors. This effect increases blood circulation while releasing tight muscles.

Types of Hydrotherapy are divided into two main categories. These are external hydrotherapy and internal hydrotherapy. It is the application of ice or water to the body. It also involves immersion of the body in water. Therefore, it aims to use temperature-based hydrotherapy techniques, such as the effects of hot and cold water on the skin and the underlying tissue. When used, hot water causes sweating and relaxes muscles. It is an amazingly effective method of treating poor circulation, arthritis, rheumatism, and sore muscles, and is often combined with aromatherapy. Cold-water hydrotherapy helps to stimulate underlying muscles and blood flow to the skin. Some of the common treatments based on water include applying moist heat to various parts of the body. This treatment with sweltering heat is referred to as fomentation. It is very useful when it comes to treating conditions like arthritis, flu, and chest cold.

Ice packs or cold compresses are used to relieve pain associated with dental surgery, headaches, and sprains. Body packs help to calm psychiatric patients and assist with detoxification. External hydrotherapy is conducted in various ways. A sitz bath is one of the most common procedures. The patient sits in a uniquely made bath where the abdomen is fully submerged in water. These baths are recommended for treating hemorrhoids, menstrual cramps, prostate swelling, and various other genitourinary conditions. There is also motion-based therapy, where high-pressure water is used to massage the body. This method is used to relieve stress and anxiety. Steam baths are also an excellent example of internal hydrotherapy. Colonic irrigation involves cleaning the entire bowel. This helps to cure numerous digestive problems and conditions. But this sort of treatment should only be recommended to you by specialists and doctors. If you happen to struggle with any such ailments, you can always advise your doctor on hydrotherapy.

The Concept of Holy Water

There's a reason why Holy Water exists. What is it exactly? It is when someone prays on the water with healing energy. It has been a concept that many may not believe to be accurate, but it does exist. It is all about transferring positive energy to water to cure another. Praying and being spiritually linked to the water transforms the effect of the water you meditate to. That's when it begins to act like a cure or medicine to any ailment or negative energy. You can pray to water for yourself to make it pure for you. Anything you place your mind or energy can help you heal or be a solution to your feeling heaviness. Just take it as therapy to flush out whatever has been bothering you. The more you have faith in the practice or cure, the more it works.

My Way With Water Meditation

As we have discussed the various ways water itself can be a miracle for you, I want to share my fun and rejuvenating water meditation exercise process. It is not only simple, but it helps you build a connection with water and take it as a source of healing that instantly helps flush out the undesired factors from your body. It has been the most effortless process for me to hold on to. Maybe you can begin with it. You can even find your way of doing water therapy that will work for you. But remember, keep it in practice if you want it to work. Keep your vibration high and concentration whenever you wish to do water meditation. You will see the wonderments that water could bring.

The Water Meditation Technique

1. Get A Glass Of Water

2. Hold With Both Hands

3. Close Your Eyes

4. Smile – this is my favorite part!

5. Tell The Water One Thing You Want To Manifest This Week

6. Tell The Water How Much You Appreciate It For All It Does For You

7. Open Your Eyes

8. Smile And Drink The Water

9. Imagine The Miracles Flowing Throughout Your Body Hanging Your Frequency So This Miracle Will Happen

With all these techniques and ways to raise your vibration, I'm sure you can better understand your system and are now able to perfectly craft a routine for yourself that fits you and your healing objectives perfectly.

CHAPTER 11

PART 1: THE SECRET PHILOSOPHIES TO LIVING A HIGH VIBRATIONAL LIFE

There are so many methods and ways mentioned in this book that will raise your vibration to higher levels. But, until now, elements were missing that would add up to a better understanding for you. When we speak of understanding, we investigate concepts, theories, and applications to adapt. The more we know, the wiser we become. We gain intelligence in terms of spirituality and higher vibrations. It evokes a sense of acknowledgment toward the most welcoming philosophies of life. It is such a beautiful feeling when we become more aware and have attained profound knowledge over any particular aspect that can help us grow. There are so many philosophies that we can apply to different areas of our lives that allow us to reflect more deeply. However, today I will unfold a couple of philosophies that I have learned throughout my journey. These philosophies are here to have you reflect and pick a path (or a combination of aspects from different philosophies) that will allow you to find your actual purpose.

Why is it essential to find your purpose? We all know that many events in life are bound to happen. We feel like we have control over life, but the fact of the matter is that our thoughts and actions are the only things we have control over. So why not give it more structure through higher vibrations and purpose? I know there are many more people like me who have struggled with severe ailments as I have, we know that life is too short and uncertain, and the only way we can make life more wholesome is by understanding and creating the best of what we have. Allow me to hold your hand and walk you through the concepts which will bring you more enlightenment. The kind of enlightenment that you need to flourish ahead while making you comprehend the tips that will serve you best—the secrets of happiness you need to manifest to become more whole and vibrational.

Ikigai: The Japanese Method to A Long and Happy Life

The people of Japan believe that everyone has an ikigai – a reason to jump out of bed each morning. According to the residents of the Japanese island of Okinawa – the world's longest-living people – discovering it is the key to a longer and more fulfilled life. Inspiring and comforting; it will give you the life-changing tools to uncover your ikigai. It will show you how to leave urgency behind, find your purpose, nurture friendships, and throw yourself into your passions.

Ikigai: Find Your Purpose

We all have that one burning desire to understand what we are meant to do in life. What is the reason behind our journey on this beautiful planet? What are we sent here to do? Is it love, or is it the vision you have of yourself to lead? This is something I would encourage my inspiring readers to think of. Were you created to follow, or were you sent to lead? Ask yourself again and again until you know what your role is supposed to be. If you were sent to lead, you were among the chosen ones with the more challenging path. Yes, the reward for you is immeasurable and intangible. You are glorious in your methods of aspiration. Don't judge your past ways; you're only human – you may not always be able to do what you wanted.

However, it is time for the good news. The good news is that every second onward from this moment is a chance for you to start again. Give yourself that liberty to start over with life if you are not happy. If there are areas that do not measure your standards, then work on them step by step. What is that key that you need to find to give you a more fulfilling life? What is your Ikigai? The answer lies all in your daily performance and what you love doing most. What is that one thing that gives you pure happiness and incites a more profound sense of passion within? The kind of passion that allows you to run to it every day. You want to chase it. What is that remarkable element that is not only unique about you but yet brings you closer to who you want to be? It can be anything, and I want you to ask yourself what it is? Once you have asked yourself all the questions that will allow you to define your Ikigai, tell me, why are you not doing it? Is it worth holding yourself back?

Hygge: The Danish Technique to Living Well

The Danish term hygge is one of those lovely words that don't directly translate into English, but it more or less means comfort, warmth, or togetherness.

Hygge is the feeling you get when you are cuddled up on a sofa with a loved one, in warm knitted socks, in front of the fire, when it is dark, cold, and stormy outside. Those are the feelings you achieve when you share virtuous, comfort-food with your closest friends by candlelight while exchanging easy conversation. It is those cold, crisp, blue-skied mornings when the light through your window is exactly right. In the evenings, that scarlet light reflects on the pages of your favorite book, which you flip bit by bit in absolute serenity. It is the way of giving yourself comfort within the uncomfortable. As we all advance further day by day, we understand that life is becoming more fast-paced and challenging. Hygge allows us to create moments that are cherishable and fulfilling to our soul.

You may think that the hygge way of life is only possible for you to have at home, but that is not true. You can have it in so many ways that can be incorporated into your work ethic. It will allow your colleagues to trust you further and give a chance to those who feel lonely and left out. It will bring your work community together and allow people to see through you and learn from you as you do the same. You will make your work experience more beautiful and inspiring.

Some methods are there that you can add to your routine and make a part of your performance. Even though it may not be in your full control to be able to convince all to be on the same page, but one step at a time, and you can make the impossible happen through your positive vibrations. All you have to do is take the first step. You can start by bringing home-cooked meals or small treats that you can bring to work. You can make cheer-up jars where each and every one writes a note of positivity and keeps it in the jar. If someone has a low vibration, they can take a note out and read it. It will allow them to feel better and have a better mood to get through the day. One must not underestimate the magic that compliments can do for you.

By performing these acts, you will extend kindness towards one another and allow one to attain a more profound sense of belonging where they work. This will raise their motivational level at work and enable them to see someplace where they can gain comfort, be it in a space full of professionals.

Lagom: The Swedish Secret of Wholesome Living

Lagom is the innovative Scandi lifestyle movement taking the world by storm. Lagom (pronounced 'lah-gom') has no equivalent in the English language but is interpreted as *not too little, not too much, just right*. It is widely believed that the word comes from the Viking term *laget om* for when a mug of mead was passed around a circle, and there was just enough for everyone to get a sip. Lagom is all about getting rid of the self-indulgent consumerist lifestyle and finding a balance in your life. We often come across that principle, which means not too little and not too much, but just the right amount. This is when one learns to be content with what he or she has. Lagom allows one to become productive within the areas of limitations that they have set for themselves as hygge may be about creating a cozy environment throughout your life. Lagom is about to make your life more manageable and fulfilling. It is the way that allows you to find balance within the unbalanced areas. You learn to see through the extra that is not required and let go of it. It is most certainly quality over quantity.

Lagom means making optimal work decisions regarding your work life when faced with challenges and demanding tasks. Wouldn't it be fantastic in a quick-moving world if you could back off and appreciate existence with less reduced pressure, but rather more an ideal opportunity for all that you appreciate and love doing? Lagom (articulated "lah-gom") is likely why Sweden is probably the most joyful country on the planet, with a sound, work-daily routine equilibrium and only experiencing requirements.

Lagom is a beautiful piece of the way of life in Sweden. It signifies, *Not very little. Not all that much. On the money.* This single word typifies the whole Swedish socially fair way of thinking on life: that everybody ought to have enough yet not all that much. At the workplace, experts who buckle down — however not to the hindrance of different pieces of their lives — are following the logo ideal, instead of consuming yourself out with a 60-hour working week and afterward getting pushed, lagom drives equilibrium and living someplace in the center. Different highpoints incorporate moderation, stress decrease, finding some harmony among work and play, and zeroing in on ecological concerns and maintainability. The core focus of this philosophy is to create such a lifestyle that brings sustainability.

Ubuntu: *I Am Because We Are*

Ubuntu is the trust in a universal bond of sharing that ties all humanity.

The concept has its roots in African humanist philosophy. In particular, the South African Zulu culture where the concept of community is the pillar of its society. Without this sense of *togetherness,* there can be no community.

Take a second to think about your life so far. These days our lives have been spent with meaningless social media connections, and our happiness is about likes and shares from strangers all over the world, yet we feel lonelier than ever. I came across the South African philosophy, Ubuntu, which teaches that all humans are powerfully unified. By practicing Ubuntu, we can fill our lives with meaning as we engage with our selfless humanity. The core principle behind Ubuntu is embracing humanity, so most of its practices focus on how to find your lost humanity.

Ubuntu asks us to recognize the humanity in others. Our perspective will change when we see what people are bringing into our lives. It's impossible to ill-treat them when you know their characteristic value. It is quite the contradiction of the new way of thinking that contrasts against each other. Whether it's a mailman or a loved one, we are no longer bound to notions like competition when recognizing their inherent value. Why should we discover others' perspectives? Most people choose the circumstances that benefit them. When we consider their point of view, we get to distinguish why they indicate it. This will let us avoid judging people built on their actions, and we will comprehend the situations better that made them do it, even if we contradict them.

The Main Secret: Consistency

What I've learned with all the philosophies, whether they are to raise your vibration or to allow you to understand life better, is that each and everything requires consistency. Yes, the key is consistency. If you are not consistent and lack self-discipline, you will not succeed in whatever practice you adopt. You have to work on it every day while ensuring that you are headed in the right direction. You have to have faith in yourself as well as what you have decided to do. Above that, you have to take a step ahead and ensure that you have been evolving. You cannot let fear or defeat hold you back. What is the worst that can happen? You may not be able to get something right at once, but you're only human. Allow yourself to go. Be a real friend to yourself that supports you and cheers for you. At the same time, be honest enough to see where you have been able not to make it. Look at those areas as your future strengths than weaknesses.

I believe in you with all my heart. It is because I allowed myself to have self-belief. If I had not done so, I would not have been able to be here speaking these words for our benefit. Yes, it was not an easy road; I have seen so much in life. But I do not regret it for a second. It brought me here to you. I wanted to take the opportunity to let you know, and you are so capable and talented. You have all the answers and cures within you. You can manifest anything you want. I know for a fact it takes a lot of courage and discipline to attain all the short-term and long-term goals, but you see, if it was put in your path, it was yours to take. This life is yours, and all of it is for you to make the best out of it. Take the chance to step up and step out, be the miracle for yourself that you wish was yours. Your time starts now.

PART 2: A LIST OF PEOPLE WHO HAVE INSPIRED ME

I wanted to thank everyone who has helped me learn about vibrational energy and healing ourselves and share with the world. This journey to find ways to live this amazing life has been a long journey. Many great leaders have helped me become a master at vibrational energy and how it works to be a healthy, more loving person. I have read so many books and studied with the best my whole life. I want to give special thanks to many great authors that have allowed me to discover the actual cure within myself. I am so honored to be able to share my experiences and knowledge with this book.

With the book wrapping up and I wanted to thank everyone that has helped me learn and share with the world about vibrational energy and healing yourself. I know I have worked incredibly hard to be where I am today, and I honestly could not have done it without my supporters. Even in the darkest of times when I felt that I could not go on with life or bear any more pain, there was always a guiding light for me waiting to hold onto tightly. I would have This journey to find a way to live this amazing life has been a long journey.

Edgar Casey VE

Healing with Light, Sound, Aromatherapy, Homeopathy, and Other Vibrational Therapies outlines energy-based therapies recommended in the readings of the renowned Christian mystic, visionary, and along with vibrational therapies employed in other traditional and modern healing modalities, as well as related scientific research.

This reflective piece allows the reader to take the best of subtle healing vibrations, aromatherapy's fragrant healing energies, the physiology of scent, the mystical lavender aromatherapy in massage baths and inhalations, last but not least, the healing with light the rejuvenating effects of sunlight light through the eyes sound as healer homeopathy.

Penny Pierce VE

As we move from the Information Age to the Intuition Age,
we need new navigating methods in an accelerating world.
Frequency is the seminal book on living in an energy-based reality.
It provides a reassuring, step-by-step roadmap into a positive
state of awareness. Inside us and everywhere around us, life is
vibrating. Each of us has a personal vibration that accurately
communicates who we are to the world and helps shape our
reality. Frequency shows us how to feel our vibration or *home
frequency*, improve it, and stabilize it as our new normal.

A simple shift in frequency can change depression to peace, anger to stillness, and fear to enthusiasm. Learning to manage our energy state can put us on track with our destiny—the life we're built for. You have a choice about the way you feel and what your life can be.

By learning to use frequency principles methods based on the way energy functions, we can keep our energy level high and productive, receive subtle information directly from the environment via *empathic resonance*, and quickly free ourselves from negative or low vibrations. The techniques in Frequency can help us succeed in the new *energy reality* emerging as we speak. Learn about the new dynamics of energy, time, and intuition. Learn the importance of unblocking the flow so you can move fluidly.

Linda West. VE

With this successful guide of ancient Theism, you can attract the right people and become more successful. You are already good at manifesting because we live in a magical world full of vibrations that you can control to create anything you desire. It is a science of spirit. You were born to use what you need to know about vibrations and frequencies that may have been holding you back.

This book is dedicated to the mastery of all your desires. The greatest gift you have been given is your imagination and passion. Everything that has ever existed and will ever exist sits waiting for you simply to love it enough to make it materialize. People often fail at the art of manifesting because they do not feel true passion for what they want. They think they want it, but there would be a love and spark that ignited the frequency to pull it in if they did. The Frequency was written to help you tap into the amazing manifestation powers you possess and how to harness and use them to get what you truly desire.

Linda West is an expert on manifesting with a large YouTube following and clients that have shared their own success stories after using her technique. If you have ever wondered why things are not showing up, you will have your answer after reading this. This book is filled with information you may have never read before about frequencies and the sixth sense science. If you do not understand the machine, how can you use it? So many people wander off into the unknown and get lost in the wrong direction. Once you have a true understanding of how frequencies work in your world, you will forever be the master of your destiny. For the good and bad, your life is dictated by the frequencies you choose to align with.

Dr. Sue Morten VE

It has long been, who am I kidding–probably always been my habit for my mind to be constantly jumping from one idea to another. I've been aware of it for a long time. This habit makes it difficult for me to stick to one idea and develop that one thing and become good.

My mind is great at multi-tasking, and in fact, has been rather ruthless and insisting in its way that I multi-task. Anyway, I am getting to making a point here. I learned a couple of the exercises which I have been doing regularly. However, as with everything else, I have wandered into other things, paused my learning, and focused on developing my energy codes. I initially read The Energy Codes: The 7-Step System to awaken your spirit, heal your body, and live your best life.

David Hawkins. VE

Dr. Hawkins developed a system for testing people's vibrational energies from zero to 1000. The average level of people across the world rests at 200. You can see the various emotions in this image. He tested Hitler to sit around 30, which means he did feel guilty, and Einstein at 499, a level of reasoning. I highly recommend the books to learn more, prepare yourself, though; they are quite lengthy and intense.

There is power in your levels. You already know how your energy affects the people around you. If not, think about entering into a dinner or a date grumpy vs. joyful and the outcomes based on your attitude that could result. Now, the other individual could completely shift your stature that evening, and that's the point. The Hawkins scale shares the science behind how positivity truly does support the planet.

Kris Karr- Crazy Sexy Cancer

Actress and photographer Kris Carr thought she had a hangover, but a Jivamukti yoga class didn't provide its usual kick-ass cure. She entered trench warfare wearing cowboy boots into the MRI machine, no less, vowing, *Cancer needed a makeover, and I was just the gal to do it!* She began writing and filming her journey, documenting her interactions with friends, doctors, alternative blind dates, and other women with cancer.

This beautiful book contains the lessons learned and advice offered from Carr's journey, as well as the experiences of her cancer posse. Full-color photos accompany personal stories and candid revelations in this scrapbook of advice, warnings, and resources for the cancer patient. Chapters cover your changing social life, dating, sex, and appearance; essential health tips on boosting your immune system; recipes; medical and holistic resources; and information on young survivor support groups. The resulting book is a warm yet informative tool for any woman newly diagnosed with the disease and for those who love them.

School of Metaphysics

I learned about holistic healing in immense depth. I went to the School of Metaphysics and read every book I could find there to learn about healing our bodies. All this came together with an understanding that it is all about our bodies' vibrational energy. We, in society, had lost this understanding a long time ago. Even though my cancer is gone, my world is amazing and filled with miracles happening daily. Each day I give gratitude for all I have been blessed with. I don't live in the past, nor do I live in the future. I live with a great love for today. I stay focused on what is important, and with this tunnel vision, it comes to me. It is utterly amazing.

Anodes Judith Ph.D. – chakra

As portals between the physical and spiritual planes, the chakras offer unparalleled growth, healing, and transformation opportunities.

Wheels of Life takes you on a powerful journey through progressively transcendent levels of consciousness. It allows you to view this ancient metaphysical system through the light of new metaphors, ranging from quantum physics to child development. When you finish reading this, you may learn how to explore and balance your chakras using poetic meditations and simple yoga movements—along with gaining spiritual wisdom. You'll experience better health, more energy, enhanced creativity, and the ability to manifest your dreams. It includes chapters on relationships, evolution, healing, and a new section on raising children with healthy chakras.

Chakra bible – Patricia Mercier

Harness the power of the chakras for healing and harmony. Chakras are the centers of energy in our body that profoundly affect our well-being. Through this exquisitely designed volume, newcomers to this alternative form of spirituality can understand every aspect of chakra power.

In addition to an illuminating introduction, a detailed guide covers each chakra, with its associated colors, Indian deity, healing stone, and emotional and physical actions. One by one, go through the base, sacral, solar plexus, heart, throat, brow, and crown chakras, as well as some newly discovered ones and chakras from different traditions. There's also invaluable information on connecting chakras with aura reading and healing and yoga exercises and meditations to strengthen each chakra.

Hand of Light – Barbara Ann Brennan

Our physical bodies exist within a larger body, a human energy field or aura, the vehicle through which we create our experience of reality, including health and illness. It is through this energy field that we have the power to heal ourselves. Only recently verified by scientists, this energy body, but long known to healers and mystics is the starting point of all illness. Here, our most powerful and profound human interactions occur, the precursor and healer of all physiological and emotional disturbances.

It is a new paradigm for the human, in health, relationship, and disease. Understanding how the human energy field looks, functions, is disturbed, healed, and interacts with friends and lovers. It informs you about training to see and interpret auras— With Medically verified case studies of healing people from all walks of life with various illnesses. You can go through guidelines for healing the self and others. The author's personal and intriguing life adventure gives us a model for growth, courage,

Forgive Yourself For Not Knowing What You Didn't Know Before You Learned It. — Maya Angelou

There are so many events in our lives where we wished they did not happen in the first place. Some so many people cross our paths we regret it our entire lives because things do not go as we had expected. We begin to hold ourselves back and stop self-loathing for not knowing what we did not. There is no other way to put it more beautifully than Maya Angelou has: Forgive yourself for not knowing what you did not know before you had learned it. Above that, forgive those as you forgive yourself.

The simplest way to forgive yourself is to extend forgiveness towards those that have harmed you. I know there are so many things that people do that leave a lasting scar on us. But it is up to us to carry those scars for the rest of our lives. We can either learn to let them go for good or hang onto them and affect our vibration. I know you have worked way too hard to balance your energy, and this is another request I will make from you. Forgive others and forgive yourself. And Forgive yourself for forgiving them because you had no other way left but to move on. You most certainly do not have to connect with the people you do not want to forgive them. It is an act that you do personally. You only need to imagine andssss pray for them. Rid your body away from the harm they have caused you, meditate the sorrow out of your system and then do the same for yourself for whatever you feel you need to forgive yourself for.

> *Forgive yourself. The supreme act of forgiveness is when you can forgive yourself for all the wounds you've created in your own life. Forgiveness is an act of self-love. When you forgive yourself, self-acceptance begins, and self-love grows.* — *Miguel Ángel Ruiz Macías*

Printed in the United States
by Baker & Taylor Publisher Services